Dancing
through
the
Storm

Dancing
through
the
Storm

Barbara Rudnicki

4 square
books

ISBN: 978-1-61766-286-7

Cover illustration by Michele Muonio.

Published 2020 by Chris Fayers under the imprint of
4 Square Books
Stillwater, Minnesota
maenadest@protonmail.com

Printed in the United States of America

Life isn't about waiting for the storm to pass.
It's about learning to dance in the rain.

Contents

Acknowledgements

So many people have influenced the writing of this book, it is hard to know where to begin. Once upon a time, long ago in the early 90s, I took a writing class from Patricia Francisco. She changed how I wrote and how I taught writing. Most importantly, she instilled a love of writing in me. She also showed me how experiences, joyful and painful, could be transformed into art on the written page.

In more current time, the writers in my Loft yearlong intensive writing class, which I took in 2018, brought the many bits and pieces of this book into a cohesive whole. Thanks to all of you: Alan Turkus, Amy Stonestrom, Anna Peterson, Daniel Hertz, Elisabeth Samson Lee, Jim Moen, Judy Hawkinson, Kelly Westhoff, Madelon Spengnether, Pamela Smith and Ryan Atwell.* Your stories inspired me as much as your encouragement and critiquing. A special thanks to my instructor Nicole Helget, whose guidance was invaluable. You knew when to push me into telling uncomfortable stories and when to praise what was working. Your two thorough critiques of my manuscript helped make this book the finished product it is today.

Along the way I must thank my family, who have turned their lifelong support of any endeavor I tried into a cheering squad for my writing: my son Louis, my daughter Christine, and my granddaughter Michele, who kept saying, "I have someone who needs to read your book". While my son-in-law Doug died too early, he had the ability to make a person think that whatever they were doing was the best thing he ever heard of. I was one of those lucky people. Then there is Callidora, my great granddaughter. While she took slummer writing classes at the Loft, I sat in the cafe and worked on my book. What a joy to share a love of writing with her.

The River Ladies, that wonderful group of teacher friends kept saying, "Isn't your book published yet?" and reminded me that, "This has been a life long dream of yours." Thank you Barbara Lindeke, Kim Corbey, Mardi Gohla, Mary Ann Hoffman, Mary Beth Scavo, and Mary Jo Merrick Locket.* We have many more journeys to take and stories to tell.

Chris Fayers came into my life by serendipity when I was looking for a publisher. He has made my first stumbling attempt into the publishing world a pleasant experience. His guidance and expertise have been exactly what I needed. Terri Evans' final editing of my book made the story dance smoothly across each page. A heartfelt thanks to both of you.

I am thrilled that my granddaughter, Michele Muonio, decided to create the book cover. Thank you for the hours you spent to make it perfectly beautiful. I love your creativity. Another thanks to my great-granddaughter Callidora who posed for the cover picture. You dance through my life.

Finally, I must thank my sisters, who journeyed through so many experiences with me and then were willing to relive both pleasant and tough memories while I wrote this book. I am so blessed to have you as my family: Mary Beseke, Patty Lefaive, and Sharon Nadrowski.*

I could write another book about so many of you who have been a special part of my life, my writing and my story. If I have not named you here, know you are named in my heart. Thank you, all of you, for taking this amazing, life-long journey with me.

*Where there is a list of names, I have mentioned them in alphabetical order by first name.

Foreword

I think I always had a book in the back of my mind. I came home from my visits with my mother and opened my computer. I wrote down those experiences, wanting the details and my emotions to be fresh, accurate. My reactions to Mom's actions would change dramatically over time. For example, when Mom ran her fingers over the picture of Pope John Paul II in a magazine, telling me how he had asked her to come help him, and that she was secretly his aide, it was a heart-rending jolt for me, a realization of her disease's progression. Later, when Mom's language deteriorated, I wished we could go back to when she could still read a few words and speak most words understandably.

When I talked about my experiences with Mom to neighbors and friends, they in turn spoke of relatives and friends who also had Alzheimer's. Story led to story: a person who saw construction workers in his back yard, a man who started a fire in his house and couldn't remember how to get out, a woman who kept sneaking out of the house and wandering. The stories went on and on. Always, people said I must write a book, tell my story, give permission for others to tell theirs. I began taking writing classes at the Loft to put together the pieces I had, creating essays instead of random thoughts. Finally, I took a year long intensive memoir writing class at the Loft. With the expert feedback from my instructor and classmates, a book finally emerged.

The story started out as my journey with Mom, her story, with my emotions and reactions to her experiences. When Mom deteriorated and no longer knew me as her daughter, I began to explore who this woman, Geri, was as a person. A funny thing happened. I also began to question who I was as a person, not just her daughter. A new secondary journey emerged, mine. At the encouragement and then insistence of my classmates and instructor during my intensive, I interspersed chapters about me. It created a unique format, with my love of dance stepping in throughout both journeys. So, here is my book, *Dancing Through the Storm*, a wee bit random and unique, just like me.

Some things I should explain. By the time I began caring for Mom, I was divorced, so you will see little of my husband in the story, except in a chapter about my married life. I did change some names to maintain the privacy of those people. Also, this is my story, told as accurately and honestly as I could. If you were to talk to my three sisters, who took this journey with me, their stories, like their memories, would be their own. We are all quite the individuals.

While your experiences with Alzheimer's or dementia might be very different than mine, I hope my story helps you on your journey and inspires you to share your own stories. Then we will all feel less alone while we struggle with this debilitating disease.

Chapter 1

When Did Your Mom's Alzheimer's Start?

Summer 2009

It was midnight. Mom stood in the corner of the hallway crying and calling "Help me." She couldn't find her way from the bathroom to her bedroom, whose doors faced each other a mere three yards apart. She was forty eight. Fourteen year old Patty, awakened and frightened, led Mom back to bed. Was this Mom's depression, mental illness, overmedication? Or, was this the first hint of Mom's encroaching Alzheimer's?

Standing by my front garden, I watched the fountain splashing water on the pink-flowered spirea bush and pastel colored yarrow blossoms. A dozen green chrysalises clung to the milkweed plant behind the fountain, their gold rings making them look more like precious beads to be made into a necklace or bracelet. Then, one caught my eye. Ever so small, a hole was beginning to form on one chrysalis, a pinpoint of black in the green. I ran to get my phone. "Pack the kids into the car and get over here right away," I excitedly phoned my granddaughter Michele. "A monarch butterfly is just starting to come out of its chrysalis on my milkweed plant."

Michele lived three miles from me with her husband Nate and her two children, Callidora (Calli) who was eight years old and Asher who was four. Michele and I had been best buds forever. As a youngster, when she was angry with her mom, she would look at her and say, "Dial Grandma Barb's number. I'm going to tell her on you." Her list of grievances most often ended with an exasperated "You know what she's like; she's your daughter." Later her mom Christine and I would share Michele stories and laugh. When she was thirteen, Michele decided we should get together once a week to write poems. "I think I had her for you," Christine once told me, again laughing.

The butterfly was halfway out into the world when Michele pulled up. We stood on the front sidewalk by the garden and watched its slow journey. Soon Asher became bored. "Can I go drive your car?" he asked. He loved to sit in the front seat in the garage, grab the steering wheel, and head into his fantasy world of driving. To the sounds of *broom broom* and *beep beep*, Michele, Calli and I watched the monarch rest on the milkweed flower, flap its wings free, and awkwardly fly from daylilies to clematis in the garden. Its bright orange color stood out on the yellow and purple blossoms. With wings finally ready, it danced around the garden like a graceful ballerina performing for us. Then it flew around the house out of sight.

"Lets get something to drink," I suggested. We got Asher out of the car and headed for the fridge where I kept Izzy pop in the door so the kids could reach it and homemade ice tea on the top shelf for us adults. While Asher played with wooden blocks and Calli got out her favorite My Little Pony puzzle book, Michele and I relaxed in our favorite rocking chairs in the sunroom. We watched the orioles and humming birds at the feeder, planned a jewelry-making day, and chatted about everything and nothing.

"I brought the kids to visit great-grandma last week," Michele told me.

"How did that go?" I asked.

"She loved seeing them. We wound up her toy walking chicken over and over and put her puzzles together with her. She had fun, but I'm not sure she knew who we were."

"Sometimes I think she remembers me as someone she's seen before, but not specifically who I am," I said. "Other times

I think I could be any stranger walking in. If I concentrate on her, and not me, it's ok. Seeing her enjoy herself is always good."

Michele nodded. "It's so hard for me seeing her like this. I think of the great-grandmother I knew growing up and the one I know now. It seems like so long ago that she was just my great-grandma. It's like one day she suddenly changed; even though I know that isn't how it went. Do you remember when her Alzheimer's started? Was there something that stood out as the beginning of her change?"

Her question baffled me as much as it did her. I tried to think back, to pinpoint the beginning. My silence stretched into what seemed like forever. Trying to find an answer reminded me of trying to find my way to my camper from a friend's home up north on a dark night. With no flashlight, I could hear noises of animals scurrying all around me, but I literally couldn't see my hand in front of my face. I made my way along the path by feel, letting my feet lead me home. Now, walking along this new path, I could catch bits and pieces of memory, but I couldn't find my way back to the dark beginnings of Mom's Alzheimer's.

"I don't really know," I finally said. "When Mom moved into assisted living in 2004, we had her tested. She proved to be low average on the cognitive scale, but scored 28 out of 30 points on the depression scale. Maybe that low average score should have been a red flag, but we were more concerned about the depression. Always, it has been difficult to separate what was depression and what was dementia. She got so much better when she first moved into her assisted living apartment. She no longer needed her walker, and her mood and physical health improved dramatically. I'd say some time during that first year we started noticing things like her forgetting to take her medicine, even when we called to remind her, and her inability to use the stove or the microwave. She didn't sew anymore, but we attributed that to a new computerized machine, which was even difficult for us to decipher. After that year, there was a steady decline."

We talked about it a bit more. Then Asher brought out his favorite Crazy 8 cards, large ones with half pirate pictures and half fairy pictures. He'd have us make up a story about each creature on each card we drew or tell what each creature's superpower was. He never won because he refused to give up his favorite cards. We spent the rest of the afternoon playing first Crazy 8 and then Spin Uno, our two favorites.

A few days later, whenever I was alone, Michele's question kept haunting me. I had been through so many stages with Mom, who now lived in a locked ward on the third floor of a nursing home. I was thankful that she had gone beyond what I called the *hell phase*, where she knew what was happening to her, where she was constantly humiliated by her mind and her body betraying her. It made her progressing dementia almost a gift for her. We would still struggle with her decline, but she was like an oblivious child, living in the present moment. I had become so used to interacting with the person she was now, working junior puzzles, playing ball, going for walks, giving her manicures, that my memories of her earlier years almost seemed to belong to someone else, another person in another lifetime.

When I talked to my sister Patty about it, she said, "I think it started long before she went into assisted living, maybe even when Mom was in her late sixties or early seventies."

I debated that it could have gone back that far, but then she reminded me how Mom had gotten lost coming home from church many Sundays. For most of their lives, she and Dad had gone to church together. Then one time he had a stroke in church. Paramedics arrived and stabilized him for an ambulance ride to the hospital. While he recovered completely from the stroke, he never recovered from his fear of where it happened and never went to church after that. Mom continued to go to Sunday Mass alone.

"She'd driven that route thousands of times," Patty reminded me, "and she still couldn't find her way home."

Mom would drive around until she'd find a spark of memory in some place or intersection, and finally get home. To our knowledge, Dad had never had to go looking for her, making it easy for us to downplay it.

"You're right," I answered. "Oh, and remember that dinner where she mixed up the ingredients for the chicken soup and the lemon pie?" At the time, we laughed at the inedible mess and ate sandwiches. Mom laughed with us, deciding she'd better make one thing at a time. It seemed more like a brain glitch of aging to us. Maybe we simply didn't want to admit to a more serious problem.

"I think Dad covered for her a lot when he was still alive," Patty continued. "They both covered for each other. Together they were able to function. I think that's why Mom fell apart after he died."

"Strange how they fought all the time, and how he degraded her so often," I said, "I remember him calling her names like *Jerkaldine* instead of *Geraldine*, her real name and deriding her for being overweight but undermining her dieting attempts. A therapist once suggested that with Mom's mental illness, his constant yelling let her know that she wasn't alone or abandoned. They had a hard relationship, yet they loved each other and, especially at the end, took care of each other." We mused how complex, and often strange, life and love could be.

That night, a memory hit me. We were celebrating Mother's Day at a restaurant. Dad was there, too, so it had been quite a while back. After dinner, we ladies all went to the restroom before heading home. One by one we gathered on the front porch of the restaurant, chatting while we waited for the others. Mom still hadn't come outside. All of a sudden, we noticed a man walking Mom out the door. She was sobbing.

She couldn't find her way out, he said. She was wandering around lost. I felt an immediate surge of guilt and vowed never to leave her alone in the restroom or any strange place again. I was also amazed. The door was not at the other end of the restaurant, but in a hallway near where we walked out, a mere two feet from the restroom.

Then there was the time my sister Sharon, on a weekend visit, took her to Target. She couldn't find Mom and was about to have customer service page her. "Just like Mom used to do when I was a child and wandered off," Sharon laughed. She finally saw Mom, pushing a cart filled with a motley assortment of items. "When did you get here?" Mom had asked, totally unaware that Sharon had driven her to the store. For Sharon, who lived far enough away to miss the weekly signs of Mom's *glitches,* this was a shocking awareness of how much she had regressed.

Patty was right, I thought. Her Alzheimer's started long before any of us were ready to admit to it. We became so used to keeping an eye on her when we went shopping, to being alert to her wanderings, that it became second nature to us, almost normal. We would never have termed it dementia, a denial in which we all colluded.

A couple of weeks after I had talked to Patty, I was having a brain MRI because of dizzy spells. It involved twenty five minutes of my head held in restraints to avoid moving it while I was in an enclosed cylinder. At first I was fascinated with the sounds and movements of the machine. After about ten minutes, however, I broke out in a cold sweat. I began to feel a sense of panic. I held the button that would call for help to get me out of this tunnel that seemed to be closing in on me. Yet, I knew that if I did that, I would have to start all over again. *Ok Barbara, you are a writer; think, think about Mother,* I told myself. I started focusing on Mother's decline after she moved to her assisted living apartment: her sewing materials scattered in odd places; her knitting, now unused, sitting by her chair; the strange things we'd find in the oven. I went on a mental tour, picturing sign after sign of her deteriorating ability to take care of herself. I was no longer panicky, but a deep sadness replaced it.

Then a picture of the dining room table flitted into my memory; on it lay a flannel blanket in the process of being tied, dark purple with vibrant, multi colored overlapping butterflies. Patty had come up with the idea. We would help Mom tie blankets for all of her grandchildren for Christmas. That way she could continue to make things like she always had; also these gifts would be a special memory of Grandma. Together Patty and I shopped for the perfect felt material for each child, ranging from light grayed purple with white daisies, to camouflage with deer. We picked out coordinating colored backing. Pinning the two fabrics together, we cut two inch strips around the edges. Every Sunday we sat around the table with Mom, talking, telling stories, tying knots, creating blanket after blanket. One by one I brought each blanket home to assure its safety since Mom had started giving things away. We tied fourteen blankets for the young grandchildren and great-grandchildren, then another seven for adult grandchildren, then another five for her children. Friends wanted some; others were donated to the church's nursery for families who needed help. Love and laughter went into every single blanket. While Mom's dementia was progressing, we had found joy in what she still could do.

When the buzzer went off for the end of my test, I was surprised at how fast the time had sped by. I came out smiling, actually relaxed. My MRI reading with the neurologist proved to be fun. He took me through pictures of the inside of my arteries, then sliced through my computerized brain image in several directions. I was fascinated looking inside my body for the first time.

"Your brain is in perfect shape, no clogged arteries, no brain shrinkage, no sign of any early dementia. Just keep doing whatever you're doing. You should be healthy well into your 90s with good, healthy cognitive ability," he said. "Whatever has caused the dizzy spells, it has nothing to do with your brain."

"I'll have to tell my sisters that I really do have a good brain; they keep telling me they think it's empty up there," I laughed.

"You tell them I said you have a beautiful brain," he said. "It's not often I get to tell a patient such good news."

I did just what he said. For weeks I told everyone I had a beautiful brain. I drove my sisters nuts repeating it over and over. To myself I kept saying, I have no signs of Alzheimer's. Although I could gradually accept that my mother had this disease, I could not bear the thought of my going through what I watched her experiencing. Teaching, writing, memorizing dance steps were vital parts of me as a person. I treasured my independence. I don't know that I could live with an Alzheimer's diagnosis.I pictured myself going out into the woods by a stream and drinking good scotch, waiting for hypothermia to set in rather than experiencing her life. For now, I was home free. The MRI and the neurologist said so.

Along the many progressions of Mom's journey, we sisters would rail against the reality of the disease, pulling our mother back into a reality where she was still our mother, could still relate to us, could still remember us. All the while she was on a journey away from us, traveling more and more into a place we couldn't follow, her new world sometimes intersecting with ours, but most often hers alone. Now we could only hope that our regular visits brought an emotional beauty and peace that lingered in her world after we left. Now on the peripheral of her life, we could advocate, assuring her the best care possible. Now it was all about her, Geri, no longer our mother, but a person who, no matter what her mind did to her, deserved to live her life with self-respect and dignity, whatever that now meant to her in her new world. For me, focusing on her journey helped me through my many emotions in losing my mother. Each step of the way, I learned to know this ever changing woman called *Geri*, alias *Mom*. When did it all start? I never could give a definitive answer. I only know it was a long, long, difficult journey.

Chapter 2

Mom Moves to Waterford Assisted Living

2004

The bright spring morning stood out in contrast to Mom's dark mood. Determined to live in what had been her home for over thirty years, she resisted moving like she had always resisted anything she didn't like. She drew her mouth into a tight line and encased her body in a wall of emotional ice. Little did she know that agreeing to move to an assisted living apartment would change her world, bringing back her health and bringing the caring love she had craved throughout her life.

On a sunny April morning, with the trees showing the slightest hint of spring's lime-green leaves, my sister Sharon, her husband Bob, Mom and I were driving to Waterford Assisted Living Apartments in their black Jeep to try to encourage Mom to move to a place where she could get help with daily living. Since Dad's death two years earlier, Mom had steadily declined, her depression increasing in intensity and her physical health deteriorating. She now needed a walker wherever she went.

Dad's sudden death at age eighty-five was a shock, even though it shouldn't have been. He had his first heart attack in his early sixties. We credit Dr. Faber for his recovery and longevity. While Dr. Faber was an excellent heart specialist, his caring concern for Dad played as big a role. Dad mistrusted all doctors and reluctantly made that first visit. He left the office as an avid follower, which only increased in depth when Dr.

Faber continued to work with him. To Dad, Dr. Faber walked on water. When he later shifted to elder care, becoming Mom's doctor, we knew Dad was right. He was as good with Mom as he had been with Dad. Dad had also had a stroke and had been diagnosed with pancreatic cancer. "It's the slow-growing kind," Dr. Faber told Dad. "You don't have to worry about it. You'll die of a heart attack before you ever have cancer problems." He was right. Furthermore, Dad's macular degeneration had progressed to the point where he saw only shadows. At my grandson's baptism, just two months before Dad's death, I sat with him in the vestibule of the church and described the ceremony. I also introduced him to people he had known all of his life but now couldn't see so he would know to whom he was speaking.

I learned about Dad's death after my final dance performance at Friday night's dress rehearsal. My son Louis suggested we sit in the back of the auditorium to talk. "Your father died of a heart attack," he told me, putting his arm around me while I shed silent tears. "He was in the garage fixing toys for the kids for when they visited Sunday for Mother's Day." We sat quietly for a while in the dark quiet, a stark contrast to the bright lights and costumes on stage, the loud music and energetic dancing. Louis offered to drive me to my parents' house, but not sure how long I would be, I told him I would be OK. His hugs would go with me. While I drove there, I thought about how Dad had died doing something he loved, something for his grandchildren.

Dad was still lying on the garage floor when I got there. "The coroner has been delayed because of an unprecedented number of deaths tonight," Patty told me. "None were related; just coincidence. The police were called in because of where and how he died. They told Mom no one could move him until the coroner gets here."

I looked at his lifeless body, his mouth open, wondering if that was his last breath out or a final gasp for air. I ran my hands through the air close to his body. I believed that sometimes a person's spirit remains, a life energy outside of the body. Friends of mine had experienced this. While Dad had been afraid of death, when he did go, he left immediately. "He's really gone," I whispered.

Only after Dad's death did we children realize how much he had covered for Mom's dementia episodes. In their final years they had become a combined unit, he balancing her dementia and depression, she balancing his physical decline. Once he was gone, we had to face how debilitated Mom had become.

We four sisters were all over the place with what should be done to help Mom. All of us could see her dementia, but what a vast territory that covered for us. Our family history might have had something to do with our divergent views. I was the first born in 1942. Eight years later, Sharon joined me. It would be another seven years before Patty was born and another four before Mary's birth. For my early years, I was an only child, then became an older sister. Sharon was the youngest but became the oldest when I went to college. Patty was the youngest, then the middle child and finally the oldest when Sharon left home. Mary was the youngest, and became the middle child when our brother Larry was born. Like the rest of us, she too became the elder child when Patty left home. That shifting dynamics was confusing enough. Mom's history of depression and our family dysfunction created psychological problems for all of us but also taught us to care for ourselves and each other. We became strong, independent individuals. No wonder we looked at Mom's problems differently. While Patty said Mom had some dementia, I insisted she was more likely in the first stages of Alzheimer's. We both agreed she needed more help than she could get at home. Mary downplayed the dementia, insisting she could stay in her home if we all helped. As financial advisor, she also looked at the benefits of home ownership for monetary stability. Finally, however, she agreed that something had to be done after her three-times-a-week visits found Mom in the same chair, crying, every time she came.

Sharon, living in Illinois, while the rest of us lived close to Mom, had the more detached perspective that distance creates. After listening to all of us for weeks, she took the initiative to get things moving. "We'll be down in two weeks to decide on a place for Mom to stay," she announced.

With a looming deadline, Patty, Mary and I visited a variety of assisted living places to try to narrow the choice to two or three during the limited time Bob and Sharon would be here. We soon realized that assisted living covered a wide spectrum from nursing-home type rooms and dingy, urine smelling hallways to clean one-room living quarters to regular apartments. We easily narrowed our list to a few acceptable places.

Once we entered Waterford, we were hooked. It looked more like a luxurious hotel entrance, two stories high, with second-floor apartments surrounding a spacious entryway. Someone was playing a piano on our left while people ate ice cream at tables in a small area to the right. In talking to the manager, we became convinced that with Mother's depression and memory problems, it would be wise to immediately have her in an assisted living apartment. While she would be OK in a senior apartment now, we weren't sure how long she could continue to take care of herself. As her dementia progressed, she would be comfortable in her routine when her memory or health declined. We all agreed. This was a place where our mother could enjoy living.

That decision led to our trip today. Only Bob could have gotten a stubborn Mom into the car. He was the one she and Dad trusted to fix their problems, their cars, and anything else that needed attention. Whatever Bob said was fact, whatever he did was golden. We sisters accepted that as our way to get things done when our parents wouldn't trust that we girls had actually grown into capable women. Still Mom resisted.

"I don't know why you're taking me there. I'm not leaving my home." Her voice sounded cold, angry, coming through tightly pursed lips. From the back seat I could picture her soft, sky-blue eyes transform to cold blue ice. I had witnessed this transformation many times in the past.

Bob escorted Mom out of the car and through the door into the lobby where we met Patty, Mary, and the manager. He introduced himself, looking at Mom. "So, you are thinking of staying with us." He held her hand and looked directly into her eyes. I was immediately impressed, having seen all too often doctors, caregivers, and store clerks ignore both my mother and mother-in-law as though age negated their ability to speak or make decisions for themselves. "Let's go sit where we can be more comfortable," he continued.

We walked to an alcove with a plush cream-and-floral couch and chairs in a circle around a dark wooden coffee table. He and I sat on either side of Mom while the others filled in the surrounding chairs. He talked about the living quarters, available activities and services, and meal options, all the while focusing on Mom while we looked on. "Would you like to see an apartment?" he asked, adding, "We have an end unit available on first floor." Mom said *yes* and off we went, the manager with Mom in tow and the rest of us following. The soft pink walls of the hallway continued the cheery look of the entryway. Railings lined either side for residents to hold on to if they felt unsteady. This was not a place where the entry was for show with the show ending once one turned into dim hallways. My positive impression increased.

The door to the apartment opened onto a spacious living area that ended in an alcove with windows on all three sides. The room was big enough to hold all or most of Mom's furniture. The kitchen was small, but big enough for the little cooking that Mom now did and with two daily meals provided for residents. A short hallway to the left led to a handicapped accessible bathroom on the left and a spacious bedroom on the right, again with a windowed alcove, large enough for Mom's sewing machine, material and craft supplies. While she no longer sewed, her sewing machine was a memory comfort for her. There was also plenty of room for her myriad skeins of yarns with which she crocheted beautiful quilts. A window on the wall by the bed added still more light, important help on her down days. A small walk-in closet finished the room, bigger than any closet Mom had had in her entire life. Satisfied, we walked back to discuss Mom's options.

"Would you like this apartment?" the manager asked Mom. She sat there, silent.

"You don't have to decide today," Mary said. "You can take time to think about it."

"She doesn't have to decide today, but realistically, this place will be gone in two weeks or less," I countered. "With Mom being afraid of heights (one of her many phobias), it could be a while before another apartment opens up. She will have to go on a waiting list. So, not deciding is actually deciding."

The manager nodded in agreement. "This one will go fast," he said. "It is one of the bigger units with the most windows."

I looked at Mom. "What do you think about living here?"

She looked down at her hands held tightly together in her lap. Her body was tense, arms tight to her sides. "I don't deserve anything this nice," she mumbled.

I looked directly at her, trying to look calm while I felt my heart constricting to contain held-in tears. Her early abusive years followed by years of her husband's diminishing her with derisive slurs, and her repeated bouts with depression had all taken their toll. "Repeat after me," I said. "I deserve every wonderful thing I can get."

"Yes," she muttered in a super-soft voice.

"No . . . Say the words after me, not just yes." I repeated

the statement with Mom very softly, hesitantly saying each word after me. "Now, once more, with feeling". She half smiled and punched me in the arm, her exasperated, yet playful way of letting me know I was driving her nuts. Still, she said the words again, this time with a little more conviction in her voice. "I deserve every wonderful thing I can get."

"Now Mom, what do you think?" I asked. "Would you like to live here or keep living at home? The choice is yours." While we sisters were pushing for Mom to leave her house, I knew that she had to agree to the move or it wouldn't happen.

"I would like to live here."

The focus shifted. Mary, who had been Dad and Mom's monetary adviser for years, now had financial power of attorney. She and the manager discussed the details of Mom's stay. She could move in within two weeks, getting the last of this month's rent free. If her money ran out, she could stay here with Medicaid assistance. Bob and Sharon would pay the initial rent, to be reimbursed when the house sold. The manager welcomed Mom to her new home. Then we left for lunch at Perkins, a long-time favorite restaurant of Dad and Mom's. They had visited so often that when their favorite waitress had become pregnant, Mom had crocheted her baby-to-be a green and yellow throw, designed for either gender. Now, the restaurant's familiarity would be comforting while everything else in Mom's life began to change.

Later we sisters discussed the sale of the house. It would entail a dumpster, thorough cleaning, and hopefully a quick sale. Having put the house in our names, 60% of the sale would go to us. The other 40% would pay for the first few years of Mom's stay at Waterford We agreed to put our percentage in a trust, with everyone having to agree on any money removed. That trust would be our assurance that Mom could stay in her private apartment with our subsidizing it when her money was depleted and she needed to switch to Medicaid. It would also provide a few luxuries like getting her hair and nails done and buying some fun outfits, even if her own money didn't last. First, we needed to get Mom moved into her apartment. Her new life journey was about to begin!

Two weeks sped by. Since I had a vision for how to arrange Mom's furniture, and since I was still teaching, I created a scale drawing to show Patty and Mary where everything fit. They approved of my plan and said it would make the move much easier. The next weekend we went shopping for a new bedroom set to replace Mom's worn out one. She chose a cream colored set with pink flowers on the headboard. A matching dresser and two nightstands complemented the bed. We also bought a new green velour rocking chair to replace an oversized chair that wouldn't fit her new space. With Patty and Mary finding some friends to help with the heavier pieces, and the new furniture being delivered on schedule, the move went flawlessly.

When I visited the following weekend, the apartment looked like home. The green leaves around the pink flowers on Mom's beige couch matched the green carpet in the living room. Her chair and recliner fit perfectly on either side of an octagonal end table in the alcove. The dining room table fit along the wall opposite her couch and next to the television set, with room in the corner for her curio cabinet, which displayed her Precious Moments collection. The end of the hallway into the bedroom and bathroom areas was a perfect fit for her china hutch. Her new bedroom furniture brightened the room. Its alcove was filled with her machine and all the materials and craft projects we could cram in. Her favorite pictures were arranged on the walls like they had been at her house. The apartment was indeed large enough that we could surround Mom with all the things that had meant home to her for the past thirty-eight years.

While Mom adjusted to her new surroundings, Patty, Mary and I proceeded with the multi-faceted chore of cleaning out the house so we could put it on the market to be sold. We first ordered the largest dumpster we could find. The basement was filled with treasures our parents hadn't been able to part with and so had been left to mold or deteriorate. We had previously done a similar clearing of the attic, a process that saddened me as I threw out items over and over that could have been sold or donated but were now trash. Once again we were hauling out pieces of our parents' lives: an old table lamp, pictures from various phases of their decorating, a broken-down wooden cabinet that my dad and uncle had made when we moved to Island Park. We planned a rummage sale with the salvageable items, knowing that with more time, glassware and other antiques could bring in more money. We simply didn't have that time. The day of the sale, the temperature rose above one hundred degrees. No one ventured out to peruse our treasures. After two days we packed up everything and took it to Goodwill.

No matter how often serendipity interred my life, I was always amazed. During the final house inspection before selling it, the furnace was condemned. It was leaking carbon monoxide. We had never thought to interfere in Dad and Mom's home maintenance, had never thought to check for a carbon monoxide detector. Had Mom stayed in her home much longer, she would have died. We rescued her in more ways than one, thanks to Sharon's insistence on immediate action.

We quickly sold the house in a seller's market. We had worked hard and fast. We said a final goodbye to a place where we had gathered for holidays and weekend get-togethers. While Patty, Mary, and Larry had grown up here, I was married before they moved in, and did not have the same attachment. We each quietly held on to favorite memories as we locked the door for the last time. Now we could concentrate on our own lives and enjoy Mom in her new life. For me that meant finishing my last year of teaching and a having a fun retirement party.

Finally fully retired, I took Mom to her doctor appointments, using those almost weekly excursions as an excuse for a luncheon date. While Mom's memory problems increased, she was still able to converse well enough that no one would suspect she had any dementia. We discovered a new restaurant in Robbinsdale, Thistles, which was on her hometown main street. The first time we ordered, the waiter came back immediately to our table. "Are you Ms. Rudnicki?" he asked. I had heard these words enough times to wonder who from my past years as a teacher would appear. When I said "Yes," he continued, "The chef is a former student of yours. He had you for Creative Writing."

I laughed and replied, "Tell him I hope it was a good experience."

The chef and I had fun talking about old times. We shared stories of his antics in class, his fun creativity and writing ability, and the cookbook he was currently writing. Luckily, he had enjoyed my class so the food was delicious. Thistle's became our favorite place to lunch.

That first year, when I came to pick up Mom for Thanksgiving dinner at Mary's, she hugged me and said, "Thank you for bringing me to such a wonderful place. I have never had people be so nice to me." She had made two new friends with whom she shared meals and activities. The staff made her feel special, especially a woman named Patti, who worked at the front desk. She and Mom chatted daily, and often she manicured Mom's nails while they talked. I helped Mom put on her coat, and arm-in-arm we headed for the car and turkey dinner at Mary's. Lifting my face slightly towards the warm sun, I smiled, thankful that this move had been even more positive for Mom than we had hoped.

Chapter 3

Who is this Woman Named Geri?

It was Christmas Eve. I was sixteen. I ran sobbing to our neighbors across the street. "Mom ran away again. I don't know what to do. What do I tell the younger kids?" I asked them. Much later, how could I, even as an adult, reconcile this fragile, depressed mother I knew with the teenage Geri I was discovering? How could she be the strength of her family, finding courage to confront a drunken father, to protect her younger brothers, to hold up her mother in grief over two sibling deaths?

A few weeks after Mom's move, three of us sisters gathered at Mary's house. Patty and I poured three cups of coffee with cream while Mary opened the box of pictures and papers that we had rescued from the basement of Mom's house during our cleaning. Knowing we could easily get distracted from our grungy job, Mary had offered to take the box home until we could spend time sorting through its contents. Coffee in hand, we gathered around the box on Mary's living room floor, eager to see what treasures awaited us.

We began by looking through pictures of great-grandparents and beyond, some we didn't know and others we barely remembered. Then we found more recent pictures including pictures of us as children. I was a wispy, curly-haired towhead; Patty and Sharon had dishwater blonde waves, a contrast to Patty's now salon-helped red hair and Sharon's thick golden curls; Mary's deep brown, straight hair contrasted to the rest of us, much like it still did. Her deep brown eyes stood out from the sky-blue eyes we other three inherited from our mother. With Dad's hazel eyes,

Mary was the anomaly, the only one with dominant genes. Old, sepia-toned or black-and-white pictures of people whom none of us had ever known, we tossed in a pile to be thrown away. Others we set aside, not sure yet what we would do with them.

While we continued browsing, a newspaper article caught my breath. On the front page was a picture of my mother comforting her grief-stricken mother. I knew about her brother's death when he was hit by a drunk driver. What struck me was my mother holding up her mother, who looked on the verge of collapse. This was not the fragile mother I knew who had been dominated by her mother. Clearly, although the grief in her eyes was overwhelmingly powerful, my mother was the strong one.

An old piece of paper lay at the bottom of the box. It proved to be an official document, a letter my mother had written requesting that my father be released from the military early because of hardship. My father worked on the AlCan (Alaskan Canadian) Highway during the start of World War II, probably to avoid the draft. He was sent home with ptomaine poisoning and immediately inducted into the army, in spite of his deteriorated health. When he reported for his physical, he was allowed one phone call to Mom to tell her he wasn't coming home. He was sent directly overseas. Because of his late induction, he did not return with the rest of the soldiers when the war ended in Europe. He was commissioned to Japan as a secretary to General MacArthur, who was overseeing the last remnants of war clean up. In the letter, Mom told of trying to care for me as an infant, working to pay her bills and trying to take care of her mother because her father drank all the money that he made. The letter didn't include what I knew from other sources. Mom had already lost their house because the low army wages were not enough to pay the mortgage.

I tried to put the timeline together, to make sense out of what I knew and what I was told. I knew my dad was at my birth in February of 1942. In her drug-induced state from my delivery,

Mom insisted she had birthed a black-haired girl. Dad had to convince her that yes, indeed, this towhead was really hers. He was inducted into the army early in 1945 and released with an honorary discharge in April of 1946. It hadn't made sense why he never completed a full tour of duty. Seeing this letter put those pieces together.

By the time we had gone through the box, I was dumb-founded. Who was this strong woman who held her family together? How does this woman, known as daughter, sister, wife, fit into the picture I have known of her as mother, a fragile woman who frequently ran away from home and who was more than twice in a mental hospital? What crushed her spirit so that she eventually couldn't cope with one more thing? I pictured her with hopes and dreams of a new marriage and baby shifting to the burden of caring for me as a single parent with occasional letters her only support from her husband. I pictured her trading her dream home for an upstairs two bedroom apartment with an oil stove in the kitchen for heat. I pictured her trying to keep her mother safe in her own upstairs apartment across the alley. I saw her finally overcome by the weight of her daily life until her only solace was the light of her sewing machine on which she created wondrous clothes, drapes and toys out of mere fabric. I heard the comforting whirring of the sewing machine motor while she worked away. That light and sound were also my constant comfort from infancy on, living with the mother who became the fragile person I knew.

Mary Geraldine Lindsay was born in 1922, twenty years before she became my mother. She always used her middle name of Geri; I never knew that Mary was her first name until after she died, when I saw her Catholic baptismal certificate. What I know of her youth comes from relatives' anecdotes. "She loved to tell stories," her brother Pat told me one day. "She'd tell them to anyone who would listen." He was the youngest in a family of five, ten years younger than Geri and ten years older than I was. I picture a young girl in her early teens with soft brown curls and eyes as blue as a clear summer sky, bursting with creativity she simply had to share. I never heard that voice. By the time she became Mom, her voice had been silenced. Her creativity shifted to her hands. She told her stories in the fabrics she sewed and the crafts she made.

Mom was an amazing seamstress. Dresses with matching coats and hats clothed me when I was a youngster. In high school, she made all of my clothes: pleated skirts, slack outfits; whatever the fashion, I had a closet filled with the latest, trendiest collection. One winter she surprised me with a sage-green suede coat with a raccoon collar. She continued to sew her children's and grandchildren's clothes, teaching herself to smock when those complex bodice gatherings became the latest trend.

Professionally, Mom had several sewing jobs. She first did piece work, which could be done in spurts with younger children at home. She made hundreds of small green giants to be stuffed at the Green Giant plant for a promotion. She made hundreds of brown sock monkeys for another store, hand sewing in eyes and hand stitching on a mouth and nose. In her advanced dementia, her brother sent her a similar monkey, thinking it would be safe and soft. She took one look at it, twisted her face into a scowl, and threw it out the door into the hallway. When her children were older, she made drapes for a friend who had a decorating business. She sewed new outfits and altered clothes professionally at home after that friend retired. As her reputation grew, she was commissioned to make pants, dresses, blouses, and in particular, wedding dresses. The most complex one that I saw required hand sewing pearls and sequins throughout the dress. From early on her sewing was her way of expressing her creativity, as well as her love for her children. It was also her safe haven, her private space in her own sewing room.

Pat shared other childhood stories with me at different times, the most riveting involving their alcoholic father. He talked a lot about how often she protected him and her other two brothers. "I remember Dad chasing her around the dining room table in a drunken rage when we were children. She would take us kids to a neighbor to keep us safe." From him and others, I heard the story of Bridget, the third child, born with her brain on the outside of her head. She lived three days. Mom told me about her taking care of Bridget in the hospital. She was the only one to see her alive. Later, in her dementia, Mom would again promise Bridget that she would take care of her, a reoccurring theme in Mom's mind wanderings. Also, later in life but pre dementia, Mom and I were making lunch in her kitchen. I don't remember what we were talking about but she paused, looked at me, and said, "I have always been so angry at my mother for always begging my father to come back home after his drunken rages."

On December 12, 1938, when Geri was sixteen, her seven-year-old brother Hinkey was killed by a drunk driver. He and his mother were bringing home wood for the stove on his sled when the driver crossed to the wrong side of the road. The force of the impact tore Hinkey out of his mother's hand. It was headline news for weeks. The driver stayed long enough to get Hinkey into another man's car and then left. The incident was deemed a hit-and-run vehicular homicide. Mom shared another painful part of the story. "When I got home from school, my dad was drunk. 'Your brother is dead. He was hit by a car.' He told me just like that and then left."

The funeral was also in the headlines, pictures of the family, Geri grief stricken, young Pat looking dazed and lost, her mother unable to walk without her husband's or daughter's assistance. Those close to the family said that neither Geri nor her mother were ever the same after that.

"Imagine what that must be like," Mary said recently when we were talking about Mom's Alzheimer's and what earlier drove her into depression and later psychosis. "Just think. Mom lost a sister and a brother in less than two years.

What if Patty and I were both killed within a few years of each other, or if you and Patty were killed. How would that have changed who we are?"

Poverty's role cannot be ignored in Geri's life. Her family struggled to make ends meet, to put food on the table and clothe the children. As Mom, Geri would get furious with my insistence on going barefoot all summer. I loved the squishy feel of hot tar under my feet. I loved the cool damp earth on the path under the forest trees. For her, going barefoot meant poverty. She got one pair of shoes for the school year. There was not enough money to buy another pair for growing feet, so summer meant having to go barefoot or wear shoes that hurt.

Later, as the young mother of a toddler, Geri again experienced poverty trying to live on a WWII soldier's salary while spending what little she had to help support her mother and father. She worked at Dayton's, a downtown department store to help make ends meet. While her hardship letter got my father released from the service early, his homecoming was still later than most other service men. By the summer of 1946, most jobs were taken by other returnees. This bright man, an accountant before the war, took the only job that he could find. He became a rubber tumbler, working on an assembly line for Minnesota Rubber and Gasket Company, a job he would have for the rest of his life.

Geri, who left a drunken, rage-filled father when she married, soon became the victim of her husband's deriding abuse. He diminished her and called her names like *Jerkaldine*. I don't remember his ever outwardly hitting her, but I saw his hugs turn to squeezing that caused her to cry out in pain. I was terrified of my spankings that got harder and harder, Dad's work blackened hands hitting over and over, me bent over watching the green linoleum floor, his angry words of warning, "Stop your crying or you'll get it harder." I would inhale deeply, holding my breath as long as I could so he would stop. Geri, now mother, couldn't handle any more. She began running away from home.

One of my earliest memories is of me crying in my crib. Rainbow colored sharp shards were flying out of my body in all directions filling the room. Then all went black as I felt myself sinking into the mattress. These intense visual images seemed to me to be an infant's preverbal expression of intense emotion. I questioned the validity of that memory until a German friend told me about almost dying when a bomb hit her buggy minutes after she had been taken inside. "But I always remember a warm, loved feeling wrapped in my blanket in my mother's arms," she said, her experience validating mine. However, I felt cold, not warm, trying to get a distant mother to connect to me.

Now, as an adult, I turned to my Uncle Pat. "Did mother ever call Grandma to come get me because she was leaving?" I had hoped that her first thought would be my safety before she ran away.

We were sitting in a restaurant he frequented, a place where the waitresses all called him *Chief* from his position as Chief of Police in Brooklyn Center. Their bantering and casual conversation showed how much they respected him. I watched quietly, looking at his sandy blonde crew cut that had been his trademark from as far back as I could remember when he would let me, his young niece, tag along on dusty alleys where the high school guys played ball. His eyes were the same sky blue as Mom's, only deeper, more thoughtful.

After we ordered, he tried to answer my question. "My memory isn't very good," he finally said. Then, halfway through our meal, he looked at me and said, "It was your landlady, what was her name? Mackenzie, Mrs. Mackenzie." I couldn't ask more. I was breathless. I had been validated; I was also devastated. In reality Mom couldn't go beyond thinking of herself when she became overwhelmed enough to run off.

How long does an infant or toddler cry before a neighbor comes to her rescue? I thought. I couldn't ask the other questions, the ones that would confirm that what I was hearing was a direct answer to my question, or whether it was a general memory out of snatches he was piecing together. I would later again question whether my memory was reality or a deep questioning after all the times I took care of my siblings in her absence.

Some things I won't ever know, can never state in black and white. What I do know is that from the day of my birth, she was no longer just Geri. She was Mom. Whatever her life was about before, it now included me, her child. It would be far into her dementia before I would once again learn who this woman Geri was, not daughter or wife or mother, but a complex person, sensitive and creative. As a child, I was devastated by her withholding love when she was angry, by her running away. I had to let go of my childhood trauma so that I could see the inner strength and courage Mom needed simply to function each day. I had to travel with her deep into her Alzheimer's before I could hear some of the stories she was finally able to share.

Chapter 4

Mom's Alzheimer's Progresses

2005-2007

It was a gradual learning process for us sisters. We laughed over Mom's bottomless hidden stash of smelly bras that we couldn't find, became fierce advocates when a new director tried to evict Mom, and agreed on one thing: maintaining Mom's dignity was all important, even when it could mean a shorter life span.

Her first year at Waterford Assisted Living, Mom improved beyond what we could have hoped. She progressed from using a walker to using a cane, to not needing either one. She attended activities and, with the help of medication for her depression, enjoyed her new life. Her inability to sew on her machine should have alerted us to mental decline, but we attributed it to the fact that she had gotten a new machine recently. While her short-term memory suffered, we were convinced that she could have sewn on her old machine because she had done it for so many decades. We kept the sewing machine, piles of material, and assorted craft projects in the alcove of her bedroom, a comfort to her and a reminder for us of her talents. Soon, however, other signs surfaced of her continued deterioration.

We noticed Mom's lack of care with her clothes when her closet began to reek of body odor. We culled out those items that couldn't be redeemed and bought new clothes, taking over the laundry care. We cleaned out two drawers full of bras, most smelling so bad that they had to be tossed. We bought her three new bras, figuring they would be enough if we washed them each week. The next time we checked, her new bras were gone and eight more old ones filled her drawer. Week three brought more old bras. We kept asking ourselves where she was getting all of the old bras when we constantly went through everything and couldn't find even one. Also, where were all of the new bras going? We couldn't find them anywhere. She had to be hiding a stash somewhere. Perhaps, like my three year old daughter who didn't like her new shoes, she threw her new bras into the garbage, hiding them towards the bottom so no one would see them. With the garbage taken away, my daughter didn't have to wear her shoes any more and Mom didn't have to wear those new bras. Finally, thirty two old, smelly bras later, we won the battle. Mom had finally run out of her stash of old bras. She had all new fresh smelling bras in her drawer, and even if many had simply disappeared, these stayed.

At first, when Mom no longer remembered to take her pills, we labeled it as simply aging or mild dementia. We called whenever she was to take them. However, when Patty went to refill her blood pressure medication, the pharmacist asked if we knew that it had been several months since it had last been refilled. Even when we had called, Mom had forgotten to take her medication. We had simply refilled the prescriptions when the bottles were empty, not paying attention to how long it had been. We decided to have the nurse at Waterford take over her medication. Even with all of the evidence of Mom's deterioration, we sisters were all over the place with how bad we thought she was, one of us asserting it was mild Alzheimer's, another maybe middle stage Alzheimer's, another insisting it was merely dementia. For all of us the label *Alzheimer's* was too disturbing a reality to fully accept.

Then came the hallucinations. First it was the aides raiding her refrigerator and watching her television when they came to check on her. Later it was the men gambling and swearing outside her window. They kept her up at night running up and down the stairs to their basement apartment. However, there were no stairs and no basement at Waterford. While I had been ready to complain about the aides taking her food, I soon realized that like there was no one outside her window, and there was no one drinking her pop. We sisters knew that there was no sense arguing about it. To Mom it was real. I understood that more strongly when I talked with my neighbor whose husband had Alzheimer's. He talked about all of the construction going on in the wetlands in back of our houses. He saw the bulldozers and other equipment and watched the buildings go up. When others tried to correct him, he stared out the back window and said, "Don't you see all that equipment? Can't you see the buildings?" We began to realize that Mom's reality drifted steadily away from ours. Her world often was hers alone.

Sharon's husband Bob solved the gambling men problem. "I'll take care of those men," he said one day when they were visiting. Then he walked out of the apartment. Several minutes later he came back. "They won't be bothering you any more," he assured Mom. "They're gone. They won't be back." She never hallucinated about them again.

At the same time, Mom sounded quite normal. If one were to have lunch with her, one would think her to be perfectly rational. We'd talk about her friends and events at Waterford and about my classes at school or my activities, all normal, every day conversations. She loved our after lunch trips to the florist for fresh flowers. She talked about wanting a wreath on her door. We found an artificial floral one for spring and summer, replaced it with a fall leaf and gourd wreath, and then a festive winter evergreen with snowmen. With each purchase she was clear about what she wanted and equally clear about how much she enjoyed her flowers and wreaths. It was easy at those times to downplay her mental decline.

Mom sounded so convincing with her stories that her doctor initially looked at Patty and me skeptically and said,

"I don't see a problem. She is fine mentally." We later talked to the doctor about her hallucinations such as the fact that there was no basement and no one eating her food. We said we didn't correct Mom at the time because we didn't want to agitate her. Gradually we established a routine during doctor visits. Mom would tell the doctor about her experiences since her last visit. The doctor would talk to her and then look at us, who were standing behind Mom. We'd shake our heads *no* when her story was an hallucination. Always, our main concern was to protect our mother's dignity.

Even with her progressing Alzheimer's, Mom continued her daily routine: going to programs, eating meals with friends, and going out for meals when we visited. We included her in all family gatherings. Then, one day Mom wandered outside of Waterford, trying to get home. To which home we weren't sure. For a long time, she remembered her most recent home in Robbinsdale, asking me to drive her by it so she could know what it looked like. We drove along Victory Memorial Drive and turned off 42nd Street to Abbott Avenue. The two-bedroom beige stucco house looked like it always had. We stopped and looked at the house and those of neighbors who were originally friends and later, when new, younger families moved in, people who casually looked out for Dad and Mom. When Mom looked at me and said, "Thank you," we drove away. It would not be long before she no longer remembered that house, but would talk about my childhood home on Dupont Avenue in North Minneapolis and later her childhood home in Robbinsdale. To her she was still living there, often the distinction between Waterford and those homes disappearing.

After the wandering incident, the nurse ordered a wrist monitor for Mom's safety, that would sound an alarm when Mom went through any outside doors. Mom cut it off. They tried a leg monitor. She cut it off. Why didn't we confiscate her scissors? We wanted to protect her dignity. Besides, like her bras, she had a hidden stash from years of sewing. Gradually, Mom became reclusive. She refused to go to meals because she was ashamed of her monitor. She became less responsive with us. Finally, we signed a release so she wouldn't have to wear the monitor, taking full responsibility if she wandered again and anything happened to her. We decided that Mom's peace of mind and dignity were more important than the safety of keeping her confined to the building. It was not an easy decision, but one we all agreed was the best one we could make. Her quality of life was far more important than her possible lack of longevity.

Mom's depression followed the same pattern as her dementia. At first, her depression lessened as she made friends at Waterford. Two women in particular became close friends, eating meals together, attending programs together, visiting each other on afternoons when no activity was planned. Then her best friend died. This friend's sister was developmentally handicapped, totally dependent on her sister. She attached herself to Mom, sleeping on her couch, spending long days in her apartment. Mom was distraught. She didn't want this person in her house, but never being good at asserting herself, didn't know how to get rid of her. The staff repeatedly took her back to her apartment, but she quickly found her way back to Mom's. Finally, the woman was forced to go to another place where she could get more supervision.

While Mom mourned the death of her closest friend, she still lunched and spent time each day with her other friend. However, I noticed Mom's depression worsening. One day I joined Mom for a concert at Waterford. We were enjoying the music when her friend came in. I stared, dumbfounded by the change in her. Her Alzheimer's had progressed at warp speed. She wandered in, a blank look on her face.

"We need to go find your teeth", an aide told her. "You are missing them again.". "They're not here?" she answered. Then she let herself be led away.

I had trouble comprehending the woman's rapid decline, but I understood why Mom's depression had become worse. She had lost her two good friends in a matter of weeks. Over the next few weeks, she wouldn't go down to eat, not fitting in at any table and not being able to ask to join others. It was like she was back in high school with the cliques avoiding those not in their group. She interacted mainly with her caretakers. Her primary interaction was with a woman named Patti, who worked at the front desk. Patti would spend hours talking to Mom while she worked. Occasionally she would polish Mom's nails. Still Mom's depression deepened.

Finally, the head nurse suggested psychiatric intervention and recommended the doctor whom we took Mom to see. At best he was weird; at worst he proved to be dangerous. Patty and I took Mom into his office because she was afraid to go by herself.

With us in the room, he spent the hour railing against all children, whose behavior towards their parents was never good. "We know how ungrateful and horrible children can be. First they are difficult to live with. Then they leave and ignore you. It's easy to be depressed with how they treat you."

Patty and I looked at it each other, our expressions showing disbelief. We were concerned enough to bring Mom here. Mom's depression started long before she had children. Besides, this man made no attempt to find out what Mom thought or how she was feeling. She barely said a word. He ended the session with a biblical quote and gave her the Bible he had read from along with a prescription to help elevate her mood.

"Who is this idiot?" Patty and I discussed later. We talked about his complete ineptitude and vowed never to take her to see him again. Still, we gave the head nurse the prescription, knowing that Mom needed something to help her through her down mood. Within a couple of weeks, we noticed Mom had put on a tremendous amount of weight. We couldn't keep food in her refrigerator. Becoming alarmed, we took her to her regular doctor, She too was concerned but would not counter another doctor's prescription. Instead she told us to keep and eye on Mom in case it got worse.

We had an appointment with another psychiatrist, one who specialized in Alzheimer's patients. He was as good as the other was bad. He talked to Mom, gave us help in understanding her problems, and recommended a book to read, *Learning to Speak Alzheimer's: A Groundbreaking Approach for Everyone Dealing with the Disease* by Joanne Koenig Coste. It became my bible as Mom progressed along her Alzheimer's journey.

"How did you get an appointment with him?" an astonished head nurse asked us. "He doesn't see patients anymore. He is training doctors instead."

We told her we didn't know why we got in. We just called and asked for an appointment after a friend recommended him. Perhaps he took us because he was training an intern who joined in the session with us. Whatever the reason, we were blessed to have gotten to see him. Still, he did not reverse the previous doctor's prescription.

Mom kept emptying her refrigerator and cupboards and kept gaining weight. One day I noticed her legs, stretched tight from weight and water gain, were weeping. I called a pharmacist friend and asked him if he would check into the drug for me. Within the hour he called me back.

"That drug is black flagged because of its dangerous side effects. Very few drugs are put in this category. It's bad stuff. Furthermore, it is never supposed to be given to older people."

I thanked him for his help, called Patty, and again signing a release so we would take full responsibility, we took Mom off the drug. Mom immediately started losing weight. Her refrigerator kept food inside. However, her depression started to return. She stayed in her apartment, not going to activities or eating. She cried often and didn't join in our conversations.

Her demeanor changed; she walked hunched over, seldom smiling. We planned more time with Mom, more trips to the flower shop, more blanket tying time. We would work naturally to elevate her mood.

Why do we give so much power to doctors? I asked myself. Patty and I knew he was a quack. Still we deferred to his prescription. We should have known better, but whatever else, he was the doctor. Why do other doctors refuse to counter another doctor's decision? Perhaps, like us, they didn't know the extent of the drug's effect. I knew that pharmacists were legally responsible if they didn't catch a doctor's mistake. They knew intimately how drugs reacted and interacted. Whatever the answers, I later wondered if that drug didn't play a significant role in Mother's future health problems. Whatever mistakes we made, we were willing to take charge, counter a doctor's orders, and help Mom regain her physical health while doing our best to work with her depression and dementia.

We could no longer avoid the Alzheimer's diagnosis. Patty heard about an upcoming workshop on Alzheimer's at the Xcel Energy Center in Saint Paul. Mary was busy that weekend so Patty and I went. We walked along informational exhibits and attended several breakout sessions. Two things stood out for me. The keynote presentation was about a nun's study. Both women who functioned cognitively normal and Alzheimer's diagnosed women had donated their brains after death. I can still picture those slides of the diseased brains. They weren't simply different. All of the sliced pictures of their brains showed huge holes, gaps in the brain tissue. I sat there close to tears, a heaviness settling around my heart. Until this time, I believed, hoped, that Mom's neurological pathways could be rebuilt, that her brain could compensate for what she now couldn't do. Some study could find a way. Looking at these slides, my hope dissipated. The growing gaps in Mom's brain were too large for her to recover.

One breakout session about how to treat people with Alzheimer's was the most helpful. The presenter would casually walk behind us and then suddenly put her arms around one of us. We watched a startled participant instinctively pull back. "That is how an Alzheimer's patient feels," she told us. She showed us how to approach so that the person could first have eye contact before we interacted. She was also the first person to assert that whatever patients saw as reality was real to them, something I already knew but couldn't have confirmed. It would do no good to argue with them, she continued. When she added that my interactions with Mom included giving up calling my mother *Mom*, I balked. I couldn't imagine her by any other name than what I had known my entire life. Every inch of me pulled back from that one part of the woman's presentation. However, I would remember that presentation later when mother looked blankly at me, confused at my calling her *Mom*. She was back beyond a time when I existed. I finally started calling her *my lovely lady*, a name we both could accept.

After another session that had nothing new to offer, Patty suggested we had gotten enough from the convention. I agreed. Over lunch we talked about what each of us had learned from the workshop. We agreed that the same two presentations that I had felt were the best were the same ones that Patty liked. What we took away from them would guide us as we journeyed through Mom's ever-changing landscape.

Throughout Mom's stay at Waterford, we had regular meetings with the staff to document Mom's health and progress. They were helpful, friendly, and always saw that Mom had good care. Then a new director came to Waterford, and Mom's money ran out requiring her to go on Medicaid. We got an eviction notice, not just from her apartment, but from the building. Bob and Sharon drove up, and we prepared to contest the decision. When we walked into the meeting, the staff looked warily at Bob. At over six feet tall, he was a formidable looking man. Little did they realize that it was we four sisters whom they had to fear. Bob would simply sit quietly and let us sisters take over the meeting.

After brief introductions, the director began by saying that Medicaid only allows a fixed number of patients per building. Their evicting Mom was according to that directive.

Mary stopped her short. "I work in this field with elderly clients," she stated. "Medicaid has no restrictions on how many assisted people can reside in a building. If there are restrictions, they are yours, not Medicaid's."

I quickly added, "We chose this place in large part because we were assured that she could continue to live here after her money ran out. It is part of the agreement that we signed."

"I am sorry, but your mother's papers have disappeared," the director countered. "There is nothing in her file."

Looking at Sharon, I knew I wouldn't want to be on the receiving end of her anger. "Then we will be keeping records ourselves." She glared at the director. "I am sure you won't mind our tape-recording these meetings. Furthermore, I think our lawyer would like to have a look at this situation."

"We don't want any trouble," the director stated, her voice a practiced, placating tone that grated on me.

"Perhaps, I will contact the news media," I seethed. "Your forcing our mother out of her home would make a good story, especially after your recent incident where a dementia resident who was supposed to be monitored walked outside, couldn't get back inside the locked door, and froze to death. Maybe that might create the trouble you say you want to avoid?" It had only been a month since the freezing incident. Another resident had switched monitors, not uncommon with dementia patients who would switch clothes, false teeth, whatever their child-like minds could think up. When the alarm went off and an aide checked, the person with the supposed correct monitor was in bed sleeping. The aide never checked further. They discovered the empty bed and the wandering woman curled up by the pond the next morning.

Patty added that she would contact channel 5 TV and I could contact channel 4 .

The director's initial confidence diminished while we spoke. Still, she sat tall and tried to command some modicum of respect. She wasn't done yet. Her next ploy was to convince us of her need for fiscal responsibility in order to keep Waterford financially sound. That didn't work either.

"Mother paid well over $100,00 before her money ran out. Since she went on Medicaid, we are paying $2100.00 a month out of our trust fund over and above what Medicaid pays you," Mary reminded her. "You are not losing any money on that apartment." She continued, "Perhaps we should have Medicaid check into your operations."

We had noticed huge supplies of rubber gloves and other general necessities on a shelf in mother's closet, leading us to wonder if she was being charged through Medicaid for supplies beyond what she could ever use. In fairness, we never checked into the matter, and had no previous other reason to expect that Waterford had anything but Mom's interests in mind. Still, at best, an inquiry would not be pleasant, and we were not at this point interested in fairness.

We were no longer the timid daughters who grew up trying to please our parents and anyone else we met. We were now four grown lionesses protecting our mother. Claws bared, we would not only fight, we would attack if we felt her safety and happiness threatened. We were not going to let this woman destroy the delicate emotional, physical, and mental balance we had worked so hard to maintain in our mother. We would not let her take away the beauty and joy Mom now enjoyed. We were also too educated on too many levels to let her bamboozle us.

The director, in a final attempt to maintain some credibility and control, excused her actions because she was new and didn't know the background. She would have to look further into the situation and get back to us. We gave her two days before we commenced our multiple actions. After cool, yet civil goodbyes, we picked up Mom in her apartment and took her out to eat. The next morning the director called Mary. Mom could continue to live in her apartment.

By the last Christmas Mom was at Waterford, we knew we would have to find another place in January. While Waterford had provisions to work with Alzheimer's patients, her increasing health issues created too much of a complexity for staff to care for her. The blank stare came more often when we talked to her. She would leave food out for hours and sometimes days and then eat it. Our grocery list had one primary requirement: would it harm Mom if she left it out. While her larder got ever skimpier, she never noticed the change. We had her stove turned off at a central circuit control. She was storing a variety of items in the oven, making it a fire hazard if she were to turn it on. She no longer knew how to use the microwave, let alone stove burners. Still, we wanted one last Christmas with her in her apartment.

We put up an artificial Christmas tree, plugging it into an extension cord with a switch so she could turn it on from her chair. We showed her how to use it. Every time we came to visit, the cord was tossed aside and the tree plugged into the wall. She had to have climbed around a chair and behind the tree to do that. How she avoided falling, I will never know. We prepared Christmas Eve dinner and rented the activity room to give us more space and let us use their ovens for our new lasagna tradition for dinner after we went to church.

When we came back from church, our activity room was decorated and full of about thirty people. Our first reaction was to evict these interlopers. Talking to the person in charge at the front desk, we discovered that the room had been double booked. Someone used the new computer system and someone else used the old hand method to book the room. This resulted in our two families preparing celebrations in the same space. We went back to the activity room to try to find a solution. They were former neighbors, which led to a brief reminiscing. We complimented their decorations. They told us the smell of the lasagna was so enticing, they'd had a hard time leaving it in the oven and wondered why it was there.

Since they had a much larger gathering, we told them we would take our food and celebration to the tables in the ice cream parlor. Reluctantly, they accepted our offer. A compromise became much easier and gentler because we were dealing with remembered friendships and a common bond in taking care of our parents.

The move proved to be perfect. The small ice cream tables and chairs provided an intimate setting. Mom relaxed while she opened her presents, chatted with us, and enjoyed her dinner. Other residents wandered in to share dessert. Our family and Mom's new sort-of family blended as we shared Christmas stories about traditional gatherings and food. Still, much of the time Mom disappeared behind a blank stare. We would later comment that we had waited too long to find another place for her. We wanted to give her one last Christmas in her Waterford home. Even more honestly, we wanted that Christmas for us, bringing back many memories of past celebrations at Mom's: caroling the neighbors; midnight Mass that later became 5 o'clock Mass; visiting the crib scene after church; a family meal, complete with suet and molasses bread pudding, a recipe brought over from Luxembourg by great-grandparents. Whatever our reasons, we created one more memory before Mom had to leave the home that all of us had come to love.

Chapter 5

Beyond Being a Daughter
My Life as a High School English Teacher

It was an ordinary adult afternoon. "Aren't you Ms. Rudnicki?" my electrician asked. My yes prompted "You had me in tenth grade. Do you know know what I remember most about you? Your were very pregnant and you loved red." So much for my erudite concept of the profound lessons I was teaching; this was an even more profound lesson in humility and a reminder to always honor and enjoy the wonderful individuality of the students in my life.

On June 9, 2004, I retired from forty years of teaching high school English, two weeks after Mom's move to Waterford Assisted Living. I made the decision to retire at age 62, knowing that by my full retirement age, I would have missed any chance to interact with Mom before Alzheimer's took over.

Ironically, my career was framed by two major national disasters. I was student teaching in Benson, Minnesota, in the fall of 1963 when news that President Kennedy had been shot came over the intercom shortly after lunch on November 22. Before the day ended, a second message announced his death. When Lee Harvey Oswald was shot on November 24, I heard it first on the radio and dashed to turn on the TV. Because of a time delay in broadcasting, I watched him walk out of the building, still alive in TV time, and tensely waited for the shot I knew had already killed him. The next day, on a small black-and-white TV, I watched Kennedy's funeral procession.

In 2001, three years before my retirement, I was on my prep period when another teacher said, "Barb, you need to come see this." I watched in horror as the One World Trade Center collapsed. Then the unthinkable happened. A second plane flew straight into the second building and it too crumbled. My next class thanked me for letting them watch the story unfold on TV. In reality, I couldn't think of any English lesson that had meaning compared to what had just transpired. Life went back to a somewhat normal routine the next day, but with heavier hearts and an awareness of how vulnerable we all were.

I graduated from the College of Saint Benedict in 1964 with a major in English and minors in speech and drama, German, and education. If there had been a degree in naivety, I would have had a major in that too. My first teaching job in Casselton, North Dakota, initiated me into the world of politics that creeps into the classroom. My first assignment was two classes each of seventh and eighth grade English, junior and senior high girls physical education, and junior high boys physical education. I spent a day at North Dakota State University coordinating my curriculum with state guidelines. Every other hour I had to change into formal classroom clothes and then back to my physical education attire. My dressing room was a basement storage room with one bare light bulb hanging from the ceiling. I draped my clothes over tables that lined the walls. The male physical education teacher had a private office which he kept locked. In it were the emergency medical supplies that I needed for my hemophiliac boy student, my girl who suffered seizures, and a girl who almost died at school the year before from a hole in her heart. I informed the parents of the student with the heart condition that contrary to what they had been told, all she needed was a doctor's note to be exempt from her phy ed classes. A month later, they thanked me, saying how much more energy she had; she could now stay awake for supper and homework.

Then I added a bowling unit, after having it approved by the school superintendent. Two weeks later a note appeared in my mailbox. *Drop Bowling.* No explanation. I took it to the principal, who was as surprised as I was. Together we confronted the superintendent after school. It seemed that the school board members' wives were sharing rumors about the unit at a bridge party. *The owner was charging students and not letting them bowl.* In reality he was instructing all of the students free to show them how to bowl before they started. *The alley was attached to a bar. Was I in the bowling alley the entire time?* The list went on and on, none of it true. The ensuing conversation went something like this: "If you can tell me one thing that is true and negative, I will drop bowling. All you have done is give me a bunch of false rumors."

"The school board has already decided; you have to drop bowling."

"Then I am going to tell the students why we can't bowl anymore," I retorted.

"You can't say anything. We met unofficially at lunch."

"Then I will tell them I am not allowed to tell them." By this time I was fuming, not caring that I wasn't tenured, only furious at the injustice of it. Once alone in the teacher's lounge, where my desk was assigned because I didn't have my own room, I kicked one high heel shoe off into the far wall, and then the other. Then I packed my belongings and went home.

Over the years, several other incidents occurred which initiated me into an awareness of the political landscape that existed everywhere I taught, although it varied from school to school. Even when I taught pregnant girls in a separate building for a countywide program in Brainerd, Minnesota, I got complaints if the girls laughed while walking around town. *Their condition should keep them somber.* I simply shook my head at such antiquated judgments. From the beginning, I vowed to keep the politics out of my classroom. I banished them to the hallway every day when I shut the door and greeted my students.

As my philosophy of teaching developed, I demanded one rule: respect.

First and obvious was respect for me. However, more important was respect for each other. Real learning could only take place in a safe environment. "What if you respect students in here because I demand it and then go after them outside of class? Is this class a safe place to work?" They agreed that no, it wouldn't be safe. "I will respect each one of you, but if I find you are disrespecting another student, you will incur the wrath of Rudnicki and trust me, you will not like it. You don't have to agree, but you need to be able to agree to disagree." Throughout the term, I could easily snap my fingers and point at the disruptor without taking any attention away from the student who was speaking. I called it my teacher finger and it worked ninety percent of the time. The other ten percent was not pretty, but usually it resulted in a truce at minimum.

There were on rare occasions, a class that I not so lovingly called *my class from hell*. Those were the classes where a teacher tried to separate the disruptive students and look each day at the good students to focus on them. In reality, I loved almost all of my students. The difficult ones were more of a challenge, but also more of a reward when I saw their excitement at succeeding. A few were exceptions.

"I think I am going to kill the teacher." His voice was loud enough for not only me but all of the students to hear. He was part of a group of tenth grade students who were known to be disruptive in school. Three of his friends were also in that class. Whispers of *Did you hear what he said? Did he really threaten the teacher?* spread through the classroom. I called in the principal. As is so often the case with teenagers, I think he said more than he meant and got into way more trouble than he had bargained for. I knew he used drugs and was probably frequently high in class. Drugs minimize control and inhibition, not a good pairing with an angry young man. He was taken to the police station, fingerprinted, and suspended from school for two weeks. He didn't return to my class.

Another time, a twelfth-grade male in combat fatigues continued to vocally counter my instructions to the class saying, "You don't have to do what she says; that is dumb." or "Just don't do this work. It's stupid." When repeated warnings didn't work, I sent him to the office with a note that said he would not be allowed back to class until he had a conference with both his principal and me. The next morning we walked into the principal's office, the student in his camouflage power fatigues, and me in my navy blue power suit.

The principal briefly started the meeting. My student immediately interrupted him. "I don't need this stupid class. My grandfather didn't graduate, and he was a successful businessman."

I looked directly at him. "Then drop English. Or leave high school. You are eighteen. If you don't need a diploma, don't stay."

He pointed at his fatigues. "The army won't take me if I don't graduate."

"Then what your grandfather did is a moot point. You need senior English to graduate and go into the army."

When the student continued to argue, the principal stepped in, "OK, I am dropping you from English. That means you will drop all of your classes at the tech school as well since you need at least one high school class and English is your only one. You are done with high school."

As his reality sunk in, my student sat there stunned. "I will go back to English."

"At this point," the principal told him, "you have to ask Ms. Rudnicki if she will take you back."

I reiterated my rule of respect. "If you can be respectful, you can come back to class. One incident and you are out for good." He agreed, with the principal reminding him of how gracious I was to let him come back.

From then on, he was not only respectful, but like other students whom I showed stern respect when they least deserved it, he became my friend and advocate. Often, I missed lunch because he stayed back to tell me stories of how he was doing in his pre- army training. I had to chuckle about the delicate balance high school seniors walk between being a teenager and an adult. Whether he was playing a game of *keep the teacher happy* or truly thankful made no difference. As Zig Zigler, a motivational speaker, often said, "Fake it till you make it." My army guy was making it.

Most students were delightful, sometimes challenging, always leaving good memories. Flexibility and permission proved to be my best teaching tools.

"Can I write about my summers at the lake instead of the assignment?" Yes. We were writing a memoir essay about their neighborhood when they were growing up.

"Can I write about how you whites exterminated us Indians just like Hitler did?" Yes. The assignment was to evaluate *Gentle Hands,* a story about a teenager who discovered that her grandfather had been a German guard in the interment camps in WWII.

The stories could go on and on. While I always felt the subject matter was important and demanded hard work from my students, equally powerful was my students discovering their own worth and capability. I also strongly believed that more learning happened in a fun atmosphere.

"You tricked us." This young lady was years beyond graduation. "I decided to work on what I wrote in your creative writing class. I never realized how much I had written. I was having so much fun, it never seemed like work."

What I considered some of my best teaching included tenth grade history/English coordinated classes for gifted students. Among many projects our first year, my teaching partner and I had the students create a *women of color in history* quilt. Ms Merrick-Lockett had annually created a quilt of paper squares on a bulletin board. She believed it was necessary to balance a male-dominated history curriculum. My wild creative penchant suggested a real quilt, along with a book of essays in which each student wrote about the chosen person. The students beamed with pride when they saw the finished quilt. When I passed around the hardbound book of essays, they ran their hands over the cover and opened it to read their own names and their essays. For two more years we did quilts. First the students created a *women in history* quilt and then a *women we know* quilt. stressing the accomplishments of women around them. The quilts and books were displayed in the high school library for several years. They are now housed at the Anoka County Historical Society, a lasting testimony to the work of those students.

College in the Schools Writing gave me an opportunity to work with students who really wanted to learn to write well before they graduated. We worked on personal and formal writing and then combined them in writing an ethnography, a study of an every day ordinary group of people as a society. I thoroughly enjoyed critiquing their papers and was continually surprised when they actually did the revisions I suggested. These were the students who in college told me that while other students were floundering, they were getting As and Bs because of what they were taught in my class. In reality, their willingness to work and learn produced their success; I simply facilitated those qualities.

Teaching requires a tremendous amount of energy. I once read that the average teacher makes over 100 snap decisions each hour. The students enervated and energized me at the same time. Even with the decreasing energy that comes as we age, I vowed I would enjoy my students and teaching until the day I retired. I did. At the end of the year, instead of organizing graduation like I had for years, I was an honored guest. I got to watch my students proudly transition into adult lives while I transitioned into my new life. Like they were ready to use what they had learned in high school in their new lives, I was ready to transfer what I had learned from my students to my interactions with Mom: respecting her, enjoying her, accepting who she was in each stage of her journey.

Today, I have a dried-up potato on my desk. When I was sick one time, two of my gifted classes signed that potato and gave it to me when I returned. Fifty-six names squeezed together in all directions. It is now shriveled, no bigger than a golf ball. The names have become wrinkles on its aged face, but the white painted eyes and smile clearly remain, a testimony to the joy of teaching wonderful, creative high school students.

Chapter 6

Mom Moves to Masonic Homes

January, 2008

It was the start of a new year and a new journey for Mom and us sisters. I hated this stereotypical, sterile, drab beige nursing home, all three floors. Little did I realize that while I learned to play childhood-like games and puzzles with Mom, I would also learn that first impressions are often very wrong

I was at Bob and Sharon's for the week between Christmas and New Years when we got a call from Patty. Mom kept getting more and more sick until paramedics had to transport her to the hospital. We had noticed her lethargic health around the holidays. At the time we attributed it to her usual December depression because her younger brother's death had occurred then. The added stress of the cost of Christmas presents and celebrations she couldn't afford always sent her mood and health spiraling downward every year. This time, however, she kept getting worse. Now her problems were so complex that it became a delicate balancing act to try to restore her health. While Mother's heart was good while she was resting, her heart rate climbed to 145 within a few minutes of her being up and walking. Add in her dementia, which worsened with even a slight cold, and it became a huge, complex problem. After brief treatment to stabilize her, the doctor refused to release her to her apartment, insisting she be sent to a nursing home for her safety and so she could be monitored by a nursing staff.

During her next phone call, Patty had more bad news. We did not yet have a nursing home with an available bed. Furthermore, Medicaid quit paying for Mom's apartment from the day she entered the hospital. A social worker was checking to find any possible place to take Mom. Finally, Masonic Homes North Ridge Center had one available bed in the locked dementia ward on the third floor. We had no choice. Unlike our earlier search, during which we found a perfect assisted living apartment, we had to accept this new place, sight unseen. She was transferred to the nursing home by medical transport. When we heard how she fought the medics going into the building, I was thankful for the social worker who took the blame and Mom's wrath, leaving us to still interact positively with her.

All of this occurred while I was still at Sharon's. Until now I had been an integral part of decision making. It was easy for Patty, Mary and me to get together for updates, decisions and care meetings. While we tried to include Sharon, it was almost always at a distance with a phone call. We valued her input. Still, it was not the same as the immediacy of our interactions. I now understood both the relief at being too distant to have to make difficult decisions, and the frustration at being too far away to be a part of those decisions. Patty and Mary had all the responsibility during this difficult transition. A short time later, I left Sharon's and flew home.

Entering the building for my first visit to Mom, my immediate reaction was *I hate this place.* It was the typical three-story sterile-looking building, my nightmare of a nursing home. I signed in at the front desk and took the elevator to third floor. The elevator opened to a large central desk, cream counters with dull-beige wood. In fact, the entire room was a drab beige dining area. Several nurses and aides worked at the desk; a few patients sat at tables. The only sound was the hum of the beverage machines.

Mom's room solidified my hate for this place. She had a small half-room by the door with a bed and a TV on a stand. Any visitor would have to sit on the bed with Mom. There wasn't even room for a folding chair. The decor was the same drab beige with a cream-colored drape between the two beds, a far cry from her spacious, well-lit apartment. This cramped, dingy space was actually no bigger than her walk-in closet in her apartment. We could look out the window to blue sky and light when we entered, but none of that filtered into Mom's part of the room.

Mom's roommate kept hollering "What? I can't hear you," every time we tried to talk to Mom. She'd further set off an alarm every time she got up, which was frequently. Aides would rush in to settle her back down in her bed. It became a timed routine that even Dante couldn't have imagined in his depiction of hell. Mom sat on the edge of her bed repeating over and over, "Please don't let them hurt me. I'll be good. Please don't let them hurt me." I held her and assured her we wouldn't let anyone hurt her. At the same time, I held my body tight, trying to keep the shards surrounding my heart from breaking loose and showing the pain I felt inside

I was sure Mom was flashing back to her electric shock therapy, which she had when she was hospitalized at age 46 with a mental breakdown. It was a crude therapy at the time, in my mind inhumane. I never got to visit her in the hospital. When she got home and I told her about my being pregnant for the first time, I was stunned that her brain wouldn't let her hold onto even that positive news. Her treatment had erased most of her previous memory, including Mary and Larry's early childhood years. Holding her now, I wondered how much that shock treatment's damage to her brain created a backdrop for her Alzheimer's. I also understood why she had fought so hard when she was transported here.

We sisters decided that Mom needed to move out of that room. After much discussion, we decided on a private room, knowing that it could also be isolating and add to her depression. Still, there could be no guarantee that a double room wouldn't produce a roommate much like the one we wanted to escape. The room that opened up was known as the Taj Mahal of third floor. It was super spacious, allowing for a table with chairs on one side of the bed, a recliner and end table on the other side, and her TV on a cabinet in front of the wall at the foot of her bed. Numerous white drawers and cupboards brightened the room. A tall oak tree stood right outside her window. Its leaves looked like a picture, changing with each season, while several tall evergreen trees formed a background. We would gladly pay extra for this room out of our trust fund. We brought her wall hangings, quilts and pictures to make her room look more like home, hopefully giving her a sense of continuity. She would soon forget her Waterford apartment, but was surrounded by *home*, hopefully her ballast as her mind and body rapidly changed.

About this time came another doctor from hell. The resident psychiatrist insisted that Mom have electric shock therapy to improve her mood. I was livid. "I have always deferred to you," I told Patty, who had medical power of attorney, "but she will have shock therapy over my dead body. More likely, over his dead body. What would be the purpose with an Alzheimer's patient? She's been through enough."

Patty agreed, freeing me from having to break my mother out of that place. We were spared an intervention when her medical doctor, Dr. Faber, intervened. We respected him and felt blessed to have him taking care of our parent. He signed a refusal for the shock therapy, agreeing that with Mom's Alzheimer's, it would do more harm than good.

After Mom adjusted to her new cheery room and surroundings, her mood rapidly improved. My first dislike of North Ridge soon disappeared. I let go of my preconceptions and biases when I experienced the nurses' and aides' caring interactions with Mom. One day while I was visiting, a nurse brought the psychiatrist in who had recommended Mom's shock therapy. "I wanted to show him how much she had improved," she told me. We talked briefly, and they left.

"Who was that man?" Mom asked.

"Just someone who wanted to see how you were doing," I told her.

"I don't like him," she stated emphatically.

"Neither do I," I assured her. We smiled in agreement and continued our visit.

Mom might not have had much memory, but she still had body memory and emotional understanding.

Patty came, bringing treats. We worked a junior 25-piece puzzle of puppy dogs. I tried to help by putting pieces close to where they belonged. If I got too helpful, Mom would slap my fingers and fit the pieces in herself. When we finished, we went to a central commons area to get Mom out of her room for a while. A TV was on in one corner with lounge chairs facing it. The opposite wall was brightly lit by two windows. Puzzles, magazines and games littered shelves for patients and their visitors. I polished Mom's nails before we left.

We were all settling in to her new home. That said, time was running out for us to decide what to do with Mom's stuff when we evacuated her old apartment at Waterford. We all knew the likelihood of her ever leaving the nursing home was next to zero. Still, it was hard getting rid of that possibility by getting rid of her things. Storage could ruin many things. We decided to divide her things among us, with the caveat that we would return everything if she ever returned to an apartment. Sharon would come down for the weekend to take part in our dividing.

You hear stories of fighting over a person's property after his or her death. I have even seen people sneaking into closets to check pockets for money or stealing items that clearly had another person's name on them. That was not our case. If anything the main problem was, *Are you sure any of you don't want this? I don't want to take anything someone else wants.* We sat in a circle on the green carpet in Mom's Waterford living room. We took turns picking out one item at a time, starting with the oldest to the youngest. Round after round we took turns choosing Moms belongings. I had appraised her rings, mostly what the jeweler called high quality costume jewelry; we divided those among us by what appealed to each one, regardless of a difference in value. At the end, we decided that we each had to continue to pick an item when what was left was stuff no-one really wanted. We laughed at each other while we watched each in turn slowly decide on some trinket to add to the more desirable pile of stuff. All along we talked about how strange if felt to be dividing Mom's belongings while she was still alive. Still, it seemed like the best plan. We cleared out everything that was left over the weekend, cleaned the apartment for the next resident, and said a sad goodbye to one of the happiest places that had housed our mother.

Chapter 7

Four Sisters Come Together

It was a summer afternoon. I was in my forties, sitting across from my sister Sharon. "My therapist said I needed to talk to people about my abuse, to let go of family secrets. I felt I could trust you more than anyone, if you are willing to go there with me." Thus began an adult bond that spread to my other two sisters.

I have often been asked how four sisters could work together so well in taking care of our mother. "Because we had to," any one of us would say. Yet it took our growing to know and respect each other in many diverse ways throughout our lives. Our age differences, our family history of dysfunction, our individual personalities, and the journey we took to get to this place in time is a story in itself.

After Sharon's birth in December of 1949, I finally had the sister I had begged for for seven years, a golden-haired, blue eyed compliment to my white hair and equally blue eyes. As she grew, this adorable little sister became a sibling who was no longer the little doll I had envisioned. We were such opposite personalities, it was hard to believe we came from the same womb. I was quiet, obedient, fearful of reprimand. She was adventuresome, active, accident prone. She spent much of her first several years in the hospital, first with rheumatic fever from her measles (I merely got an eye astigmatism), then with a concussion from falling off a retaining wall, then from swallowing a pin. Even as adults, I'd call her with my latest craft project, while she would delight in a vintage part for the '57 Ford hard top retractable that she and Bob were restoring.

She was science and math; I was literature and mythology. Reading *Zen and the Art of Motorcycle Maintenance* awakened in me an understanding of her spirituality and how similar we really were at our core. Gradually, as adults, we became close friends as well as sisters, delighting in and complementing each other's uniqueness.

Seven years after Sharon, Patty was born in December of 1956, when I was in ninth grade, my first year of high school. She was sensitive and caring, wonderful qualities, but ones that crushed Patty's spirit when Mom would run away from home or when Mom would have nervous breakdowns. We developed a close older/younger sister relationship. As adults, our similar personalities and mutual interests gradually turned that relationship into a friendship where age difference melted away. Being the practical, organized one among us random thinkers, she needed timelines and details, a definite bonus for whatever decisions and actions we needed to accomplish with Mom.

Four years after Patty's birth, on a sunny August day, along came Mary, just as I was about to enter college. She was more like Sharon. The young father whose beatings I feared was the older father Mary feared would succumb to a heart attack or diabetes. Where I would cringe under his stern reprimands, Mary would learn to most often dismiss his gruffness. He would still lash out but no longer had the strength of his youth. She and Patty were opposites, much like Sharon and I were. However, their closer ages made them interact more like siblings, the fighting, the sharing, even into adulthood. One day I said to them, laughing, "You are such sisters. You still fight like kids. Patty, you need to be organized and plan, while Mary flies by the seat of her pants, organizing things at the last minute." They looked at me, startled, then agreed and we all laughed. We also teased Mary about her Pollyanna outlook on life, threatening to paint a gondola over her garage door with the words: *Queen of Denial*. Still, we all loved her positive outlook when we needed a boost.

Three months after my wedding, and four years after Mary's birth, Larry was born in November of 1964. Our age difference spanned twenty-two years. I never knew him as my brother. He was instead a playmate for my children when we came to visit. He later became a big brother helper for his nieces and nephews, much like Uncle Pat had done for me. Whether because of four strong-willed, intimidating older sisters who had been like part-time surrogate mothers to him, or because of his need to personally work out his trauma with Mom, Larry did not join us four sisters in our care of Mom. I thought back to when I finally sought counseling to heal my demons and learn to set boundaries. I was in my forties. Larry was in his forties now, perhaps needing a similar timeline. He would forge his own path while we four sisters worked together.

In 2004, Sharon found A Place in the Woods near Bemidji, Minnesota, and said we sisters should go there for a weekend; we needed time together. In early October the resort traded fishing weekends for a planned women's retreat.

Mary called me the week before our scheduled stay. "Would you be willing to do a fire ceremony while we are at the resort?"

My spiritual path had taken many turns including chakra energy work and sweat lodge ceremonies, a year-long shamanic fengshui study, and performing fire ceremonies, primarily to release old difficulties and bring in new, positive life experiences. While Mary remained a strong Catholic, she respected my journey and our family's many intuitive gifts.

"I have been having this recurring dream where the Blessed Virgin Mary keeps telling me to go into the woods and consecrate my family to her. She says I am not to worry; she will take care of everything. Then when I wake up, I keep thinking of a fire ceremony to do what she asks."

I agreed to plan for a ceremony while we were there. We drove up on a Friday afternoon, arriving close to sunset. The sun sparkled on fall water, a bit darker and thicker than in summer. Leaves rustled under our feet sending up a dry, lightly musty smell while we unpacked the car and settled into our cabin. Pine wood walls and rustic earth-tone plaid furniture welcomed us with their coziness. After supper, we walked by the lake, headed back to our cabin and soon were ready for bed.

Saturday filled with planned and optional activities. We each signed up for a massage in the morning. When it was my turn, the therapist said, "You are a dancer, aren't you?" When I told her yes, that I had danced throughout my life, and was currently clogging, she replied, "I could tell by how tight the muscles are in your legs." While she worked out knots on my entire body, she told me about the time she did therapy for a dance convention. "I was exhausted by the end of the weekend. I don't think I have ever worked so hard on so many people with tight legs." At least I was the only dancer in our group.

The afternoon was designated for making fall centerpieces out of small pumpkins. We each hollowed out a pumpkin and then filled the hollowed-out space with artificial fall leaves and berries. I looked around and wondered how a few decorations could create such different looks. Our cabin filled with the scent of pumpkin emanating from our strategically placed art work.

After supper on Saturday evening, I prepared a fire ceremony for the four of us. I stacked the wood and started the fire to let it settle down before we started. Then we gathered sticks, acorns, leaves, and anything that called to us and made symbols of what negative aspect of our lives we each wanted to release. Patty and Sharon wrote release words on paper. I tied dead leaves and twigs together. Mary had already brought her one item, a rose for the Virgin Mary. She planned to release all negatives and let her namesake Mary take care of the specifics.

Quietly, each in our own thoughts, we set our individual intentions into our creations.

When we gathered by the fire, I created a cornmeal circle around us to provide a protective barrier, asking that only helpful spirits and angels cross into our circle. Then we began. I asked the spirits of the fire to help us release negative energy to make room for positive experiences in our futures. Mary asked the Virgin Mary to bless us all in this endeavor. While each of us knelt to toss our hand-made symbols into the fire, the other three formed protective angel wings behind her. Then each one reached over the fire and pulled smoke around her, filling her space with room only for future good and leaving no space for the negative to return. At the end, we sat around the fire and watched it turn to glowing embers.

To this day I credit that weekend for bringing us sisters closer. That closeness would help us make difficult decisions along the path of Mom's care: differing, discussing, compromising to give Mom the best final years we could imagine.

Chapter 8

Mom's New World

2008–2010

It was late at night. I sat in my sunroom and sobbed the tears that I had held back trying to be strong. I felt devastated at the continued loss of the person I knew as mother and guilty that I was glad for her progression into advanced Alzheimer's, for the childhood innocence it brought her. Gradually, I let my mind picture the joy-filled memories we had created along the way and fell asleep.

"Barb, can you come help me?" Mom stood in the bathroom, shit running down her legs, clinging to her pants which were down around her ankles, covering her shoes and the floor. My first reaction was a *why me* revulsion, *why not Patty?* A memory flashed through my brain of a long ago time when my children had called *Mom!* every time they wanted something. I jokingly said I wished they had only learned to say *Dad*. Like I had done with the kids to help calm them, I once again braced myself and put on what I hoped was a neutral face. I began cleaning the dried defecation in the folds of her aged butt and thighs, thinking how ironic it was that I was now changing the woman who first diapered me.

My revulsion at the smell and mess changed to compassion as I listened to my mother's sobs. How humiliating, I thought. Her body and her mind are both betraying her, stripping her of every dignity while she stands naked and helpless in front of her daughter. I got her out of her clothes and slowly washed her everywhere with wet paper towels until I could see no more mess. I handed a clean mother over to Patty to dress and comfort while I put her clothes in a bag to be laundered, cleaned her shoes, and then cleaned the bathroom. I washed my hands three times, remembering previously changing dressings when an infection in the crease below her breasts contained e coli bacteria. Standing at the bathroom door, I watched Patty lying in bed next to Mom, stroking her hair and talking gently to her. Mom looked totally devastated and exhausted. I felt totally helpless. Then, seeing the lavender lotion on her counter, I did the only thing I could think of. I began massaging Mom's hands and arms, feeling her muscles slowly relax. I handed the lotion to Patty who massaged her other arm. Mom's deep shudders from her sobbing slowly shifted into a steady, relaxed breathing. When we left, she was falling asleep. I leaned down, kissed her forehead, and whispered, "Next time I come, I'll bring nail polish and we'll do your nails."

A few weeks later, another mess. This time Mom looked at me and in a childlike voice said, "Oops, I messed." Gone were the tears and humiliation, replaced by an acceptance of shitty clothes that reminded me of a toddler being potty trained. Mom had crossed from what I called the "Hell Phase" of awareness into a new world that held the simple mind of a child. She left behind her humiliation, her fears, her depression. She began a journey that more and more held only the present moment. She left me behind in my own parallel journey, trying to cope with a disease whose world I couldn't understand, a world that terrified and mystified me, a world that took my mother further and further from me. Even though I knew this was a huge leap into her Alzheimer's, I was thankful for the new innocence that this hideous disease had given her.

We soon established a routine visiting Mom. Patty and I would go on a weekend day together and Mary, and sometimes her daughter Candace, would visit on a weekday after school and work. If possible, one of us would try to fit in another day. I routinely manicured her nails, using a warm wet cloth to wipe the cuticle remover from her fingernails and rubbing lavender lotion onto her hands and arms. Then I'd let her pick from a variety of pink colors, avoiding reds which too easily showed the flaws in my finished product. Every visit, we wound up a toy chicken that waddled across the table, never failing to delight Mom. She had us wind it over and over again, clapping her hands and laughing gleefully every time.

Mary often came about suppertime, visiting Mom while she ate. On one of Mary's visits, Mom's plate was barely touched, even though it was close to the end of the meal. While we had a notation that her food needed to be cut for her, her plate was set in front of her like all of the others. Mary took the tough skin off the chicken and cut it for her. "It was so tough, I had trouble cutting it," she told me. Once the food was in smaller pieces, Mom snarfled it down like she was starving. However, Mary observed, "She doesn't know how to use a fork. She pushes her food around the plate, not knowing she could use the tines to get her meat."

The nurses had informed us at our last care meeting that Mom wasn't eating most of her food lately. After talking to Mary, I thought back to when they told us that she *refused to take her pills.* I was visiting Mom when they brought her two pills, put them in her hand, gave her some water, and left. "I don't know what to do with these," she said. "Let me help you," I told her, gently putting the pills in her mouth and telling her to drink them down with her water. Patty called her social worker the next day, emphasizing the difference between refusing and needing assistance. This latest food incident would require yet another call. Our constant vigilance combined working with caring, yet human caregivers and monitoring those who didn't do their jobs. As Dr. Faber had told us at our first meeting, when we were more visible, her care improved. People treated her with more respect because we did, and because they knew we would be vocal if they didn't. Whether good or bad, it was a reality we worked with, all the while aware of those who didn't have advocates.

Mary called me one evening, telling me about the oranges that were served at supper. "What are they thinking serving oranges to a locked floor dementia ward? I shouldn't make fun of the residents, but you should have seen it. No one knew what to do with them."

Everyone at Mom's table was rolling the oranges around, pounding them, and trying to figure out how to get them open. Some were throwing them like balls.

"Drop them hard and smash them," one resident told the others, "and they'll explode open."

Mary peeled Mom's orange, took off any stringy substance that she might choke on, and made sure there were no seeds. Mom then shared her orange with the others, who exclaimed over their sweet juiciness. Mary peeled more and more oranges for everyone to share. Five oranges ended up in the garbage for lack of time to peel more.

"I'll bring you some tangerines next time I come," Mary told the ladies.

"Wait until you taste those," one woman exclaimed, her face beaming with memory and expectation. "They're even sweeter than oranges. I love tangerines."

Mary took Mom back to her room, leaving a group of joyful ladies at the table, all because of a peeled orange and a bit of common sense caring.

Always, new developments with Mom surprised us. One day, when Patty and I arrived, she was walking along the hall. She knew both of us as her daughters that day, greeted us with hugs and kisses, and was truly happy that we were there. We brought hot cocoa, as much for us with our below zero weather as for Mom in her well-heated room. We also got an apple fritter, one of her favorite treats. While she ate it, she chatted on in her usual rambling repertoire of stories about children, men, money, her dad, and shopping. More and more she spoke mush when no words came, where she used to substitute some word that came to mind. She also tired after about an hour, compared to the two-plus hours she used to enjoy. Incidents like this continually pointed out her mental decline, one to which we had sadly become accustomed. However, we were not prepared for the scenario when we handed her the newly washed pink teddy bear.

Mom looked at it briefly. She inhaled a deep breath that forced her chest abnormally out and then shuddered an exhale. At first, I thought she was having a heart attack. However, she calmly looked at the bear, said a few words, and went into a trance-like state. She started revisiting her early life in iambic poetry, four or five beats to a line. Mom's voice was so soft we at first couldn't determine what she was saying and thought she might be reciting a poem. Patty looked at me, shocked. I motioned for her to turn the TV way down. Listening carefully, we picked out something like the following pattern.

I promise you that I'll protect you
I want to take and show you to your mother
But they don't want to let her see you now
I promise you that I'll protect you
Your dad has not come home yet
But I'll take care of you when he comes home
I promise you that I will always protect you.

For seven or eight minutes, she talked more clearly than we had heard in over a year, all in the same poetic verse, pausing briefly at the end of each line. At times I felt like she slipped into the time of my birth, when my dad left to work on the Alcan Highway and then was drafted into World War II. Then, her story seemed to travel further back in time. I knew enough facts to understand what she was talking about. Her only sister was born with her brain on the outside of her head, possibly from when my grandfather had pushed my pregnant grandmother down the basement steps during one of many violent arguments. The doctors advised against my grand-mother seeing her baby like that. My mom was the only one to see her little Bridget alive, and took care of her in the hospital for the four days that she lived. It was also Mom, the oldest child, who frequently took her younger brothers to neighbors' houses for safety when their dad went on a drunken rampage. At twenty, she felt abandoned to take care of me, and perhaps my birth brought back those traumatic days with her sister.

While Patty and I could only catch a fraction of what Mom said, we both knew that this was a trance-induced revis-iting of her early life, all in clear, poetic language. After about eight minutes, Mom blinked, looked at us, and said, "You're still here." She was exhausted, returned back to her usual lack of language, and was ready to rest. We covered her, settled her in her chair, and kissed her goodbye, the pink bear still in her arms.

"I'm freaked out by this!" Patty said. "Should we stop her, hold her hand, what? I want to help her, but I don't know how."

"Wherever she is, it's her private journey," I said. "We can't go with her on this one. From what I know of trance states and out-of-body experiences, we could do physical, emotional, and/or psychological damage if we try to physically intervene. She is not disturbed by what happened, nor does she show any signs of distress. Maybe we're the ones who need help more than she does."

We continued talking, trying to make some kind of sense out of what had just happened and assuring each other about what we had witnessed. We both wondered if her episode was one step closer to death. That thought brought me to tears, ice cream, and television that night.

My questions continued to haunt me. Mom never read poetry or anything beyond women's magazines and directions for patterns to sew and crafts to make. Where did this obvious poetry come from? If Alzheimer's resulted in physical loss of her brain, leaving holes that could not be repaired, how could she suddenly be so clear? Did she memorize poetry in school, as Geri Lefaive, that person who was not yet my mother? In my teaching of poetry, I always started the unit by discussing how poetry expresses the inexpressible. Was Mom finding a way to express what in life were experiences she seldom talked about, and emotions that were suppressed by a husband who couldn't handle her sadness? Was this trance-like state a way for her to cope with a horrific childhood and over-burdened teen years? While I would probably never have answers to these questions, they gave glimpses into my mother's life separate from me. I grieved the loss of the woman I have known as my mother. I honored the woman Geraldine, whom I was only beginning to know as her own person. I wondered at the small gifts this disease brought in the midst of the devastating losses it inflicted.

I was sitting by the fireplace reading a mystery novel when Mary called me one evening. I could tell from the sound of her voice that she was upset.

"Mom was really agitated when I got there."

"Really?" I questioned. "We had such a good afternoon. We did puzzles, she talked gibberish a lot and seemed really happy and contented."

The afternoon had gone well. I got out one of her junior puzzles, the one with Pluto the dog on it. She had done that one over and over until I no longer had to match pieces for her to put together. She laughed and brushed my hand aside if I was putting too many pieces together, laughingly threatening me with her fist. While we worked, I listened carefully to one of her muddled stories, one I hadn't heard before.

"I almost got hit by a car today," she said. "I was walking home when one car was speeding down the road. It hit the other car and sent it right towards me. It hit me . . . well, it didn't hit me; I got so excited I lost my footing and fell down. Some nice young man helped me up. 'How are you getting home?' he asked me. ' I don't know. I guess I'll have to walk like I was doing,' I told him. 'You're not going to walk after that fall. I'll get you home.' So he took me home and here I am."

Mom had gotten to telling rambling stories, some I could relate to like when she talked about the staff taking her to meals or activities. Or the time she had her purse dangling from her walker and told us about going shopping at Dayton's. Or the time when we had taken her to my daughter Christine's for lunch in Saint Cloud. Christine gave Mom a *Martha Stuart* magazine. Mom ran her had over the cover and said, "I worked for Martha Stuart. I really liked it. But I don't know why she hired me."

"She hired you because you both have the same interests. You both are amazing cooks and seamstresses." Christine told her.

"Oh," said Mom. "I don't work there any more. I don't know why."

"You retired. Remember?"

"Oh, yes."

That ended the conversation. We ate lunch, and then brought Mom back to her third-floor world.

I couldn't tell where other stories came from, or what was based in fact from her earlier life, what came off the TV, what came from a place in her mind we couldn't fathom, or what combination of all of these. I'd carry on conversations like they all made sense, often leaving my sister Patty staring in awe at the bizarre interactions that ensued.

"I don't know how you manage to keep up those conversations or begin to know what she's talking about," Patty would marvel.

"I think it comes from teaching teenagers for forty years," I'd laugh. Perhaps it was my penchant for writing, often making up conversations. Whatever the reason, I had a knack for conversing with Mom when I had no clue what she was talking about, often not even sure what I was talking about.

When I left her that day, I put on a DVD of *The Honeymooners*, one of the old TV series which she remembered and enjoyed.

"What was she so upset about?" I asked Mary. "She seemed settled when I left."

Mary shared her interaction with Mom.

'What's wrong Mom?'

'I am so frustrated. I can't remember.'

'What can't you remember?'

'Was I ever married?'

"Barb, I didn't know what to tell her. She seemed like she really needed to know. So I told her *yes*."

'I can't remember him,' she told me, so I got their wedding picture and showed it to her.

'See, this is him. His name is Bob.'

'What happened to him?'

'He died about five years ago.'

'Oh, I thought something like that had happened. How long were we married?'

'Over sixty years.'

'It couldn't have been that long.' Mom kept shaking her head *no* and saying *not that long*.

"Barb, I didn't know what to do or say," Mary repeated.

"Don't worry about it." I reassured her. "You did the right

thing. She really wanted to know and understand. You can tell when she is and isn't in her story world, the same as I can. You knew she needed real answers. You did something very special for her tonight."

After we hung up, I sat alone in my sunroom, wondering if *The Honeymooners* had sparked some memory of her and Dad. I debated whether the DVDs of Red Skelton, Dean Martin and Jerry Lewis, and George Burns and Gracie Allen were a comfort to her or whether they stirred memories that agitated her. Not being able to enter her mind, it was impossible to know for sure if what we did was right. All I knew was that they brought a spark of joy and laughter when she watched them. Perhaps that was enough; perhaps the couple's arguing brought back memories of Dad's negative behavior toward her; perhaps seeing their youthfulness in the episode brought memories of earlier years when they swam and picnicked together. The sepia-toned wedding picture showed a tall handsome man and slender, beautiful young woman, their eyes sparkling with hope. Now he was dead and she was losing her mind. Knowing how that hope and joy slowly, steadily evaporated weighed heavily on me.

The next week when Patty and I got to Mom's room, she was sitting in her recliner. She beamed when she saw us. I had brought some more of her clothes and gave her the choice of which to keep. I noticed clothes on the bed and hanging on the closet handle and checked to be sure they had her name on them, wondering why they were out. All were labeled, so I assured Mom that after the staff had put her name on the clothes, they would bring them back. Once again, I explained that she needed her clothes marked with her name so that the people who washed them would know that they were hers. She looked doubtful, like she had no choice but to trust me. This possessiveness had become normal to her with everything, even her puzzles or toys.

Minika, Patty's ten-year-old granddaughter was with us. Together, we all looked at the family pictures we had taken for Mom's 85th birthday. We talked about who each person was, who were families, and of course, how we were her favorite daughters, a long standing joke going back to forever.

"That's my son," she said, and we affirmed "Yes, that's Larry," casually giving her a name that we knew she had forgotten. Then we talked about his wife and the children, again reminding her that they came every Friday to see her. These prompts hit places in her memory that led to stories, some based in fact and others coming from places we once again couldn't understand. This ritual started with Mary's gift of her family memory book, complete with pictures and captions. Patty, more that the rest of us, made sure to go through pictures every time she came. It was one way we hoped to activate as much of her memory as we could for as long as possible.

"I think I'm going to move back to Minnesota," Mom said. "I can't find my husband here. He doesn't come around any more."

"Your husband died," Patty told her. I thought back to Mary's visit. Obviously, this had been on Mom's mind.

"He died about five years ago," I added.

Mom looked at us, a spark of grasping that fact flitting through her eyes, a tinge of sadness before she lightly replied, "Oh, not that one. The one who's been here." In her mind she had many boyfriends, the staff who took her for walks to meals becoming dates. The time factor varied from when she was younger to a present day coquettishness when she talked about how she had to shoo them home. I wondered how much might relate to her actual dating years, a time about which we children knew nothing.

"I don't know what to do. They treat me well here. Still, sometimes I want to go back to Robbinsdale." This trying to find her previous life had become a new pattern. A couple of weeks before she'd snuck on the elevator, telling the people at the first floor desk that she was going back to Dupont Avenue North, where we lived in the 1940s and early 1950s. Another time she was going shopping at Downtown Dayton's.

"Everyone loves you here," I said. "They all say wonderful things about you."

"Besides how would we know where to find you," added Patty. "We'd be sad if we couldn't come see you. I think you need to stay here."

"Yes," she said. "I think I'll stay."

Patty and I picked up her clothes and put them back in the closet, realizing that she had taken them out to leave. Much of her bulletin board keepsakes were missing, too. Having been through this type of packing or hoarding with her before, I knew the places to look: her Kleenex box, her jewelry box, her candy tin. Noticing her puzzle boxes, I shook them. They were filled with her treasures. Sometimes she seemed to be "cleaning" and other times putting her things in special places. This time she was *packing*. My constant frustration was never knowing what was in her mind. It had become a strange land that I could not navigate.

I'm not sure who got out the orange ball, one of those soft ones with knobs all around the outside, so enticing that even the nurses couldn't resist playing with it when they came to check on Mom. We played catch for a while when Patty's granddaughter Minika got the idea to play basketball. We opened Mom's drawers and took turns trying to get the ball into them. The scoring got more and more elaborate, using four drawers, then adding her wheelchair, a nook beside the TV, and under the drawers. The additions came when Mom couldn't get the ball where she aimed. Basically any place her ball landed was a new "basket". The scoring was also designed with a three point system so that Mom, or maybe Minika, would get the most points. We laughed and giggled until our sides hurt. During these times of Mom's pure delight in the moment, all of her years battling depression, all of her memories of abuse, all of her fears and sadness disappeared.

"This is the happiest I have ever seen Mom," Patty reminded me one time when I was really down about her Alzheimer's. "It is a gift from an otherwise horrible disease."

Playing ball that day, I had to agree.

When we got ready to leave, we put on a *Red Skelton* DVD. Mom showed me the case, which had her name and room number on it. "I knew him," she said, weaving a tale about how they met and how she worked with him. "See this," she said pointing at her name and room number on the case, "R. . M. . 123. That's our secret code. And he autographed my name for me. See," she said pointing to her name.

"That's really special," I told her, smiling. There was nothing to be gained from correcting her. We were about to leave her in her own world, one in which Red Skelton could actually be a friend.

Mom walked to the door and watched us walk down the hallway. At times like this, I felt guilty leaving her. I turned around one last time and waved at her. She waved back. The memory of her standing alone in the doorway in her impenetrable world followed me home.

That night, I cried once again, the joy of playing ball, knowing she lived happily in the present moment not enough to counter my deep feelings of loss. I had worked hard in therapy to accept my mother's frequent rejections by running away or refusing to talk to me for weeks or months at a time. I had concentrated on the ways she could show love by her sewing and cooking. I had set my own boundaries which allowed me to enjoy my mother more as an adult than I ever could have growing up. Now, Alzheimer's was taking that away from me. And to be honest, I still felt responsible for her emotional well-being, just like I always had from as far back as

I could remember. It wasn't fair. I took a deep breath and dried my tears. It did no good to wallow in what I didn't or couldn't have. I still had Mom in whatever capacity she could interact. I let the memory of her sparkling eyes and broad smile and the sound of her laughter during our visit today tuck me in for the night.

Chapter 9

Third Floor Care Meetings

2008-2009

Thinking about the doctors we had encountered, I pictured the movies The Good The Bad and the Ugly, *doctors riding a desert landscape of health care on wild horses. We had had our share of bad and ugly doctor care._Now we not only had the good, we had the best.*

About a month after Mom settled into her new room at Masonic Homes, we had our first conference with her doctor, her social worker, and the head nurse. Patty, Mary and I got to the room first, a small room right across from the elevator. It was the usual drab brown with three cushioned chairs and one straight backed chair. Obviously they weren't used to several family members attending these conferences. Sharon had often laughed when we told her about our conferences at Waterford. "Are you sure you all attended the same meeting?" she'd ask, it being obvious that our take and what we each remembered varied significantly. I told her we would telephone conference her into the meeting. There was no phone in the room. I spotted a black wastebasket, took out the plastic lining, turned it upside down, and placed it in the center of the room with my phone on it.

When the three professionals entered, they looked at the wastebasket and then looked at us with quizzical, wary expressions. My logical explanation of its purpose kept them from wondering whether we should join Mom here. They brought in chairs from the dining room for themselves. We had the comfy chairs; first come first served. We were thrilled to learn that Dr. Faber would continue to be in charge of Mom's care. Our Mom was in good hands.

I dialed Sharon and introduced her to each of the staff members. The meeting started out with our reminiscing about Dad with Dr. Faber. Then I asked him, "Is that your Porsche in the parking lot with the oldie doctor license plates? He laughed, his blue eyes twinkling, making his roundish face and sandy hair look more like that of a schoolboy than an accomplished doctor. He said, "Definitely not. I was raised in a working-class home. My parents would have a fit to this day if I did anything that ostentatious."

It was time to get down to the meat of the meeting. Dr. Faber started with a metaphor to describe Alzheimer's. "Imagine," he said, "that you take 35W to work every day. Easy. Then it is detoured because of construction. You find a new route. That route goes under construction. Then more and more construction until you are lost trying to find a road to work. What was an easy commute becomes next to impossible. That is like your mother's brain. More and more her ways of thinking are blocked. Sometimes she is lucky and can find her way. Most of the time she is lost, her brain unable to navigate uncharted territory." I thought of the summer when so many of our roads were under construction that when WCCO news gave a list of blocked roads, they said, *And if you live in the Coon Rapids area, we suggest you take a helicopter to work.* We had laughed at their method of escaping those frustrating roads. But Mom could not lift out of her tangled brain. She had no helicopter.

Dr. Faber put Mom's current mental capacity at about the age of a three-year-old. We talked about her progress and how she was settling in to her new home. Periodically, I would ask Sharon if she could still hear all right or if she had questions.

When it came to a *do not resuscitate* order, we were all hesitant. We didn't want drastic measures, but we weren't ready to give up if she had something like pneumonia. She had recovered from that before. Dr Faber suggested a compromise. He would order one round of antibiotics. If that didn't help, he would switch to palliative care. Sharon was particularly concerned about not feeding her and wanted a feeding tube. In our Catholic upbringing, denying Mom food could be considered sinful, even murder. To all of us it seemed cruel to add starvation to a dying person's pain. Dr. Faber explained that not eating is part of the body's dying process, its way of gradually letting go of this life. He further discussed how painful feeding tubes could be. "Once you order it, you cannot change your mind," he cautioned. We left that issue to be determined when the time came, all of us now leaning towards letting nature take its course but still hesitant. After discussing a few housekeeping details with the nurse and social worker, our meeting ended. I told Sharon we'd call her later, hung up the phone and put the plastic liner back in the wastebasket. Then we went to visit Mom. At our next regular meeting with just the nurses, a phone sat on an end table by one of the chairs.

In September of 2008, we had our six-month conference with the doctor. Sharon was here from Illinois, her first in-person meeting. We joked that it seemed strange not to have the wastebasket upside down. Dr. Faber once again went through the stages of Alzheimer's and what to expect. He put Mom's mental capacity at about 18 months, down from the 30 to 36 months that he had estimated at our last conference. It seemed like too much of a progression of the disease, too rapidly. Yet, when I thought about it, I knew that she kept losing more and more vocabulary, that her sentences were more often phrases, pauses where words eluded her.

I could picture Mom during the parts of the memory test that I knew. Five words: *apple, car, church, house, tie;* the words varying but always a sequence of five. She would maybe remember one right away, and going back after a conversation, she would remember none. She would stare blankly as the doctor told a story and asked her questions about it afterwards, unable to comprehend what was for her too much information at once. Drawing the face of a clock would be a frustrating, impossible chore. There were many more tests, the final diagnosis left up to her doctor. I knew Dr Faber's age determination was accurate. It was simply hard to hear it put in stark numerical terms.

Dr. Faber noted that she was beginning to aspirate her food, not much but enough to signal another progression of the disease. He suggested eliminating foods such as nuts and hard candy. Even her Jelly Bellies could be too small and hard for her to swallow. As far as her appetite, she was eating well, especially sweets. Dr. Faber said there was no reason to deny her this simple pleasure. We could bring her pastries and her favorite Dairy Queen hot fudge sundaes. Her weight was holding steady, a good sign. "When a patient loses interest in or capability to eat, they start losing weight. When they lose about eighteen percent, we know that the end is near." I wondered who came up with that magic number and who gave it such importance. I vowed to bring Mom enticing sweets whenever I visited, as though I could postpone the inevitable.

We talked about the Christmas season and what to expect. The doctor agreed with our recent decision that large crowds such as our gathering at her place for birthdays were becoming too much for her. Visiting over several days in small groups of two to four people would be much less stressful for her. Again he reminded us that it would be more for us, since she would forget we had been there within minutes after we left. While I already knew this, it was difficult to hear it again. This Christmas Eve, we would not be going to Mass with Mom and gathering at her place afterwards. Mom would no longer be making Christmas cookies with us the weekend after Thanksgiving. Those traditions were already lost in the tangles in her brain. Her place in her favorite rocking chair or at the head of my table would remain empty.

"What would you give as her life span?" Mary asked.

"I broke my crystal ball last week," Dr. Faber joked, then said "Seriously, if I were to guess, I would say that she will be with you for Christmas. I doubt that she will be here next summer."

My entire body contracted at the reality of those words. I had often said that I wished and prayed that she could just fall asleep and not wake up, that she wouldn't lie in a vegetative state for years like my friend's mother. Now, I kept thinking, *I lied; I don't want her to die. Whatever kind of life we have with her is better than nothing.* Dr Faber would prove to be right once again. His crystal ball was broken. Mom would be with us for many more years.

We briefly discussed hospice care when the end was near and our options of leaving her here or moving her to a hospice shelter that might be better for us. We opted to leave her here where she has been comfortable. While we were ending the meeting, I once again said a prayer of thanks for this doctor who was both caring and knowledgeable, whose foremost concern was Mom's welfare, not doing drastic measures to keep her alive, but assuring that she would be as healthy and comfortable as possible. Whatever procedure he did would be here at the nursing home, rather than further confusing and agitating her by sending her to an unfamiliar and terrifying hospital. Whatever our mother's future, we all agreed that we were more confident and relaxed knowing that Dr. Faber would be taking care of Mom.

By March of 2009, the meetings were becoming more routine. While the doctor's meetings seemed more vital, we kept in close contact with the nurses and social worker on a regular basis. When Patty couldn't make one meeting, Mary and I made it a priority to be there. If nothing else, we all agreed with Dr. Faber that the more the family was involved, the better the care.

What we learned during the meeting confirmed our observations during our visits with Mom. Her cognitive ability had deteriorated significantly. Her last test score was a 14; this time it was a 4. I didn't understand how this test worked, or the numerical system it used, but the change was drastic. I was surprised at how this information hit me physically, creating a churning in my stomach, a sadness close to tears, and a heaviness of spirit. I also wondered who came up with this definitive, black-and-white numbering system, even if it were correct. I had noticed that Mom's lack of vocabulary had increased. Also, she no longer tried to remember a word, saying things like braid for spine or waving the unknown word away with her hand as she moved on with her talking. Her focus had also diminished. She could not sit still to have her nails manicured, something which she used to love. I now geared how much I did with her nails to her tolerance level at the time. When she talked, she skipped from topic to topic, seldom finishing a train of thought. For us sisters, whose conversations had always skipped around because we knew what wasn't said, our inability to track Mom's stories surprised us. While the numbers told us nothing we didn't already know, to hear about her decline in technical terms was again difficult.

The psychiatrist had reported that Mom was having more psychotic episodes, a harsh term, making me think of someone who was severely mentally handicapped. It also made me like him even less than when he had suggested shock therapy for Mom. He really did not understand dementia. I told the people in the meeting that what he called *psychotic*, we referred to as her *fantasy world*, a much gentler term. However, I could not deny that she often heard something totally different than what we said, saying things such as "Did you hear that? He wants to know what those boys did with my money." We may have been talking about doing a puzzle, the plant in her room, or some other mundane conversation. More and more she was in her own world, acknowledging us, talking and playing with us, yet somehow placing us in her own reality at the same time.

The social director called Mom *Ger Bear,* a testimony to how much she was loved by the staff. Mom enjoyed them and the attention they gave her. She usually went to gatherings such as music time or bingo, even winning at times. Recently, however, she got up halfway through an event and walked back to her room, unaware of the activity going on around her or that she had been a part of that activity.

As always, my consolation when we ended this meeting was that Mom was unaware of her deterioration, and she was mostly happy and cooperative. I wanted so much more than this for her and prayed that she would not end her life uncommunicative, existing by lying in a bed, not speaking, not reacting. That I had no control over that made me fearful, angry and sad. I tried to concentrate on her smiles, her joy at playing ball and doing puzzles with us, and what bits of herself she offered us in her ramblings. The last time I had come to see her, she was walking in a hallway on the far side of the floor. When I walked up to her she smiled and said, "It's been so long since I've seen you."

"I was here last week, remember, Mom."

"Oh yes," she smiled.

This time when I hugged her she gave me a long, strong hug back.

"It's so good to see you," she said. "I always love seeing you."

I have cherished the memory of that moment, one moment of sunlight in the darkness Alzheimer's often continued to create.

Chapter 10

Christmas Celebrations Change

2008

It was Christmas 2008, the first time Mom could no longer be at our preparations and celebrations. We all felt the empty hole her absence left. More shattering, when she hit me at the end of my visit this Christmas. How could I suddenly be transported back to childhood trauma and its horrible emotions? How could a tree lit holiday suddenly turn black?

During the 2008 Christmas holiday season, we faced our first time without Mom at our celebrations. Dr. Faber suggested that it would be traumatic for Mom to leave the building, even for a short visit. She would be disoriented wherever she went and would again be disoriented when she returned. We acquiesced, with some misgivings. Then, one day when I was looking for Mom, I saw an aide walking with a sobbing woman. *Her family took her home and now she doesn't know were she is anymore,. Why don't you walk with us?* she asked me. They were walking the hallway towards Mom's room, so I joined them. When we got to her room, Mom wasn't there. I handed the sobbing woman one of Mom's stuffed animals. While she cuddled it to her, she stopped crying, its softness a comfort to her. I understood what Dr. Faber had been talking about with Mom's possible disorientation if we took her home. All misgivings disappeared when I shared this incident with my sisters.

Our cookie baking this December was filled with laughter and powdered sugar everywhere, my nieces Candice, Minika, and Kaemaella and my nephew Kavante creating wonders with frosting and rolling hundreds of balls to be made into 13 different kinds of cookies. Last year Mom had sat in the big chair at the head of the table, rolling balls of cookies, drinking diet soda, at times drifting off, but then returning. This year her chair remained empty, keeping her memory present even though an emptiness lingered at the table, a twinge of loss in the midst of the mirth.

Mary called me in tears a few weeks later. "How can I make the cranberry salad if Mom isn't here to help me?" Mom's cranberry salad was almost as historical a tradition in our family as was the suet pudding, a molasses bread pudding served with a butter sauce that made the rich dessert even richer. I had watched Grandma, Mom's mother, make it every year, telling us how her mother had made it in Luxembourg and had brought it to this country when they immigrated here. Mom later was assigned the pudding task and now me. When I once suggested trying a lighter dessert for a change, I was told in no uncertain terms that it was my duty as the oldest daughter to keep making the pudding. Some traditions cannot be altered, like some ingredients, such as the suet that my home-town butcher wrapped in a red bow each year, a vital ingredient because of its slow dissolution throughout the pudding.

While Mom's cranberry salad wasn't as ancient a tradition, it had gone back as far as our memories could take us. When Mom could no longer keep recipes straight in her head, she would go to Mary's and together they would recreate the recipe. I'm sure it must have been written down at one time, but we never bothered to get it from her. Besides, Mary could remember the recipe and would have no trouble recreating the cranberry salad. This wasn't really about that at all. This was more about the many days where an empty space lingered in Mary's Christmas preparations. She had taken over the Christmas dinner after I moved farther into the north-lands, a drive that nieces and nephews found too far when they had other places to go. Mary's place was centrally located, easy access for those who could only stop in and inviting for those of us who spent the day. When mother could no longer prepare her own holiday events, Mary took over her shopping, inviting Mom over to wrap presents. Mom helped clean, and of course helped make the Christmas salads. Mary was feeling a loss, more deeply in the everyday activities than the rest of us because she had been more intimately involved with Mom's part in them.

As Christmas approached, I found that I was exception-ally organized gift-wise. However, I hadn't bought anything for Mom. When I talked to my sisters, I discovered that they hadn't either. What do you give that's meaningful, yet something that she would enjoy? Patty was going to get her some new tops; Sharon would get her a new necklace that she could put on over her head; Mary decided on a soft troll-like doll for babies that sang lullabies when you squeezed it. I decided that I would get her a hairbrush and products to counteract her cradle scalp, a brush type curling iron, and new nail polish. A small reindeer on a sled that sang and moved in circles when you squeezed its hoof seemed an easy enough toy and one that she would enjoy.

Christmas morning, I woke up for my first Christmas alone, weather keeping Sharon and Bob from coming home for the first time that I could remember. Since my divorce, they had stayed at my house, and Santa had never forgotten to fill our stockings. Now their absence would be added to Mom's. I had spent Christmas Eve at Patty's house with her family, another first. Mom's house had been the place for Christmas Eve celebrating for years. Even when she was in her assisted living apartment, we'd make all the food, put it in the oven, go to Mass, and then come home to celebrate. The routine was the same this year, only Mom wasn't a part of it.

Patty's daughter Nikki stopped at an open drugstore on the way home from church to buy me a box of candy. She didn't want me to be the only person without a gift when their family opened presents. Her thoughtfulness touched me deeply. We had a wonderful evening, the children entertaining us with a violin repertoire and singing. I was struck with how traditions continue, modify, and carry on. It was like Mom was already gone, even though she still lived.

In the morning I sat by my Christmas tree, the fireplace on, sipping coffee and reading my paper. The tree sparkled with hundreds of multi-colored mini lights. Ornaments from as far back as the seventies crammed every branch on my eight-foot Frazier Fir, creating what I called my memory tree. The oldest dated ornament, from 1978, had a choir boy who turned under a wooden frame. The orange and gold bird I had made in the early seventies, when orange and gold and avocado green were the in-style colors, tucked into a middle branch. Ornaments the kids had made in grade school hung next to years of delicate glass ornaments. Every one had its own story, its own memory.

Memories from my childhood included a fresh cut tree equally loaded with ornaments; silver tinsel hanging from every branch reflected the multicolored lights. Each year Dad made us hang the tinsel one strand at a time. Our furtive efforts to throw a bunch on a branch brought a stern demand to take them off and put them on the right way. After Christmas, we would reverse the process, carefully taking down each strand and looping it over a piece of cardboard to save for next year. I eagerly woke up each Christmas morning, the early morning chill in the house and my excitement bringing goose bumps and shivers Of all the gifts of dolls and games and toys, the most memorable was a Brothers portable manual typewriter, green keys on a black body, all tucked into a carrying case, ready for my senior high school papers and my fall trek to college.

This morning held solitary fireplace warmth instead of chills, and a peaceful joy from my reverie. I would go to see Mom this morning, fix her hair, and manicure her nails. Patty would come later with her clothes and stay for lunch. Dr. Faber had advised that it would be too unsettling for all of us to go at once, so we planned times that would fill her holidays, trying to space things out so she wouldn't get too overwhelmed or tired. I kept thinking how much like any other day Christmas is; we are the ones who put so much emphasis on it to make it special. It wasn't a sad awareness, just one more difference in an ever-changing landscape.

Mom delighted in opening her bag of goodies, but kept saying, "Christmas? It can't be Christmas." Even though the decorated and lit tree had been in her room since Thanksgiving weekend, even though tinsel and a wreath adorned her walls, it was one more connection she couldn't make. We played with the reindeer for a while, her delight contagious, dispelling my sadness at her inability to remember how to push the hoof to make it work. She'd be successful a few times; then she'd bat it around, expecting it to somehow work on its own. I got us some juice from the dining room, not having planned on Caribou being closed so we couldn't get our apple fritter and turtle mocha. I worked her scalp with the soft natural bristle brush, creating a blizzard of dead skin. Still, hard, dry flakes clung to her hair, making combing it difficult. The curling iron calmed her hair, giving her a soft style. She picked out the bright pink nail polish, and I was just finishing her nails when Patty and her friend Mike arrived.

I sat back and watched them take over, Mike giving Mom two beautifully wrapped boxes. Mom looked at them, turned them over, and stared, not knowing what to do with them. Patty finally took them, unwrapped and opened them, and then gave them back to Mom to do the final pulling back of the tissue paper. She delighted most in a beautiful silk, gray-and-white top with sequins glittering throughout the material. That is the one she decided to wear. We finished getting her dressed, including a touch of lipstick. She was ready to celebrate as much as her disease would let her.

When I was getting ready to go, I turned my head to find my coat. Mom hauled off and slugged me on the back of my head. Hard. Painfully hard. Head jerking hard. Hard enough to hear a thud.

Mike stared at me with a surprised look on his face. "What the . . . ? Are you all right?"

Patty, busy adding decals to Mom's window hadn't seen anything. She turned and looked at us, confused.

"Your mom just hit Barb!"

I stared ahead, fighting back tears. I was immediately back to being her child, back to the many moments of her rejection, back to the many slaps across the back of my head from my dad when I couldn't sit still enough. I put the candy back in my purse that I was going to leave for her. "Have a fun lunch. I'll see you at Mary's later," I said as I turned toward the door and left before I could start to cry. I knew I was behaving childishly, but I also knew I was reacting viscerally, that I needed time and space to regain my adulthood. The sense of loss, the many changes, the held-in sadness spilled over in tears while I started my car. I felt guilty for being angry at her, childish for not being able to control my emotions, helpless in time's unrelenting toll on my mother, afraid of what time had in store for all of us. I calmed down on my drive to Mary's for dinner, realizing that Mom's reaction was probably more that of a petulant child who, while the adult in her wanted all the attention, had been made to sit still too long for hair and nails, who couldn't make presents and toys work, who was feeling as overwhelmed by Christmas as the young child that her mind made her. She acted out to release her pent up frustration. Or . . . she was mad that I wasn't staying for lunch, her more adult self reacting more personally to my not doing what she wanted. Once again the horrible dichotomy of this disease eating away at my mother's brain, creating an adult with a child's mind, hung heavily on me. Once again I agonized at my inability to know what was going on in her mind. In an instant, I had been transported back to childhood, when she would run away from home, when I would wonder what I had done wrong, the raw guilt and fear not far from my adult self. I was angry at me; I was angry at her; and I was angry at being angry. And somewhere in that anger was a shame I didn't want to admit to or face. I would visit Mom the next Sunday; I would work puzzles, throw the orange ball, and make her toy reindeer sing and go in circles. She would not even have a memory of the incident, or that I had been there Christmas day. In reality, her actions were not memorable for anyone but me. Life and her disease continued on, just like any other day.

Chapter 11

Family Dysfunction

When one understands everything, one can forgive everything.
—Budda

My brief regression into childhood that Christmas of 2008 brought back many painful memories over the next several days. How does a person define family dysfunction? Webster's Dictionary defines it as a disturbance in the function of a social group. Roget's Thesaurus doesn't even attempt a synonym. Siri states that the synonym of dysfunction is dysfunction. Dysfunction is dysfunction is dysfunction. Crazy making. Even I, who experienced it, couldn't break it down into a single definition or condition. Its reality shifted with mounting experiences. Its only constant was the harm it did.

Frustrated, I created my own definition, trying to capture its dichotomy. Dysfunction is a den of dragons lurking on the landscape of an average family who are trying to live a good life. They sniff the smell of fresh baked caramel rolls for breakfast. They listen to the progress of piano notes from *Twinkle Twinkle Little Star* to Beethoven. They peek in late-night windows to watch a piece of blue, black and white material turn into pedal pushers for a special school picnic the next day. They watch the man and woman fill a box with meat and home-canned food gathered from what little the family had, to be given to a neighbor whose husband left her with two children and an empty refrigerator. All the while, these dragons sneak around the periphery of the house, scoping out each person's weaknesses, fears and angers, deciding which dragon will infiltrate and attack which family member, plotting to destroy the family. These dragons gradually succeed. Family members end up isolated in the smoke from the dragons' fire, unable to see each other's struggles, fighting for their own survival.

Living the complex dichotomy of seeming normalcy and dysfunction, I think of my childhood years as fire and ice: the fire of my father's rage and the icy rejection of my mother at any minor misbehavior. Dad didn't beat up Mom like her father had done to her mother. Still, he was mean and abusive. Mom often became overwhelmed and ran away, crying "I can't take it anymore." Dad would look at us children and say, "Now look what you made your mother do." I was devastated, trying to figure out what I had done that was so wrong.

One memory that sticks in my mind happened when I was sixteen. Mom had refused to talk to me for weeks, her usual punishment when she was mad at me. I exploded. Screams of rage and pain flew out of my mouth, as I threw my hairbrush, curlers, books, a mirror, anything I could find. Grandma hit me on the back of my head, not with the rage filled eyes of my dad, but with eyes full of fear and concern. Grandma later apologized and told me she loved me. Mom started talking to me again. My life went back to normal, at least what I knew as normal.

The first time Mom was put in a mental hospital, I was in high school. I took care of Sharon and Patty and tried to keep the household functioning. When Dad discovered that I could make really good fried chicken, he insisted I make it over and over, just in case that was all I could do. He was trying to hold his life together by controlling the only thing he could, my cooking. He couldn't handle even the thought of my making a food mistake. In many ways, daily life went on much as usual with school, homework and play time. It was not much different for me than the many times Mom ran away for a day or two, to where, we were never sure. In some way this was even better. It was not the frantic helpless feeling of our family falling apart. It was not the terrified feeling of not knowing where she was or if she would again come home. This was doctor ordered; it would make mother better. However, Mom's hospitalization didn't help for long. Nothing seemed to change.

One summer day shortly after Mom got home from her second hospital stay, Sharon called me crying. I was living nearby with my in-laws during the summer of 1966 and waitressing at Lafayette Country Club to supplement my teaching salary of $2700 a year. Patty had left the freezer door open and mother was threatening to run away. Could I come over? I could feel Sharon's desperation in the sound of her voice. Many times when I was a teenager, I would run to the neighbors, sobbing. I had felt responsible to hold the family together but totally incapable of doing so. I had also felt a deep fear of my world flying apart. Now Sharon was bearing the same burden. The scene when I got there could have been a sit-com if it weren't so tragic. The first thing I saw when I entered was Sharon, sitting at the breakfast table on the porch crying.

"Hang in there," I comforted her. "It will be all right. Take a deep breath and sit here while I go talk to Mom." I hugged her and proceeded to the living room where Mom was on the verge of taking off.

I set Mom's packed bag aside and hugged her. "Lets go see how bad things are," I said. "Maybe we can save some of the food."

I called Sharon and together the three of us went downstairs to the basement. The freezer door was still part way open. No one had thought to close it. We got rid of some fish and bread. Everything else was still frozen and salvageable. What could have been a simple solution had become a devastating tragedy. Mom was now calmer. She would stay, which calmed Sharon.

I next found Patty in her bedroom sobbing, "I'm making Mom run away. It's all my fault."

"It's not your fault," I told her. "Accidents happen to all of us." Let's go for a walk and talk. The summer day was sunny and warm. We walked along the wooded path by our house, the tree leaves creating a lime green canopy that softened the light and cooled the path. I repeated over and over that Patty had done nothing wrong. We all had done something like that at times. The problem was Mom's depression. I'm not sure she totally believed me, but she started to smile. We left the woods, walked one block along the hot tarred road, and turned right towards towards the lake. At the end of the dock we sat down, dangling our feet in the cool water. By the time we headed home, Patty had relaxed and we talked about afternoon swims at Chester Park swimming beach, which was an easy walk from the house. When I left, the family had resumed their normal daily activities, Mom baking, Sharon and Patty coloring. I, on the other hand, relaxed only after my own private down time.

The second time Mom was hospitalized, Sharon became the caretaker of Patty and Mary, and a new baby boy, Larry. Where I had witnessed Dad's abuse of Mom, Sharon is haunted by the memory of Dad at his workbench threatening suicide, one hand on the gun laying in front of him. Bills were piling up, bill collectors kept calling and threatening, Dad felt helpless to take care of the family. She pleaded with Dad to stay alive and said she would take over the bills and the household. At age 17 she balanced a budget, called bill collectors to tell them how much she would be sending them each month, and wrote out checks for all the bills, forging Dad's name. At the same time she maintained an A average as a senior at Saint Margaret's Academy while taking care of her younger siblings. That meant many absences from school.

"You will have to take senior year over," the dean told her during a meeting. "You have too many absences. Making exceptions wouldn't look good for the school."

"How would it look if it got out that I maintained an A average with barely any instruction from your teachers?" Sharon countered. "That wouldn't look good for the quality of your education, would it?"

Sharon graduated with honors. However, with Mom in the hospital, no one attended her graduation. I baked her a cake to celebrate, not the party she deserved, but at least a recognition of her success.

Four years after my wedding, Sharon married Bob and moved to another state. By this time I was living in Brainerd with two children. Together Patty, Mary, and Larry formed a family, much like Sharon and I had. By this time mother's depression grew into psychosis. She would tear the house apart and try to get the kids to call the police and tell them their dad did it. They lived in fear of her, never knowing when she would have another episode. Dad was yelling more as his life became less and less in control. In the midst of everyday life, the house filled with tension. I felt it when I came to visit, a presence so thick that I felt like I had to cut through it to get into the house. When I left, I could physically feel a weight lifting off of me, a weight the others couldn't escape.

One year, Bob and Sharon stayed at my house for Christmas because our parents' basement was too damp for Sharon and had lead to bronchitis the previous two years. Christmas morning, we ate breakfast by the tree and checked to see what Santa had left in our stockings, some wonderful gifts, and a little snowman poop (miniature marshmallows) for when we had *misbehaved* during the year. "It's so peaceful and quiet," Bob commented, like he was waiting for some commotion to begin. In contrast, during previous holidays at our parents' house, Dad yelled and hit the kids, the kids cried, yelled and frantically tried to get dressed on time, and Mom was stressed and in tears, frantically rushing to get ready for company. This year, we enjoyed a relaxing morning and had plenty of time to prepare Christmas dinner for the entire family. Commotion was not invited to our party.

Several years later, life came crashing down on Patty when she and Mary went to the corner store for candy. Mary ran out into the street and was hit by a car. She was in critical condition in the hospital. Dad and Mom blamed Patty for not watching her more closely. The "look what you did" with the freezer incident was nothing compared to this shaming. While they sat by Mary's side during her recovery, Patty was left isolated, feeling the weight of their judgment on her, feeling her own sense of guilt. Mary soon recovered; Patty only began to heal as an adult.

Afterwards, I could see that Patty was barely functioning. When I offered to have her live with me for the summer, Mother told me that she would rather see her in a foster home than with me. I took my parents to court. When we entered the small room, the judge was already sitting behind an elevated honey-colored wooden barrier. If the neutral beige colored walls were meant to create a calm atmosphere, it didn't work for me. I was shaking inside and had to work to keep tears at bay. I knew that this encounter would at best lead to another round of Mom's silent treatment.

The judge looked slowly at each of us. "Tell me why you are here."

I took a deep breath. "My parents and sister are not getting along. I would like to have my sister live with me for a while to give them all time apart." When it came down to it, I didn't have the courage to ask for permanent custody. Perhaps that kept my parents from contesting my demand. Perhaps it made the judge's decision easier. At least that is what I told myself when I felt guilty for not asking for more. The judge granted me custody for three months without any further questions.

That summer with Patty was a fun three months. We enjoyed the relaxed atmosphered of ordinary days: gardening, baking, swimming, playing with my two children. Then, in August, Dad sent his mother to talk Patty into coming home. She couldn't say *no* to her. Neither could I. Patty was fifteen, old enough to make her own decision. I didn't have the courage to further tear apart my relationship with my parents. I couldn't face another court appearance. Patty went home.

After school started, I began getting phone calls, waking me up at two or three in the morning. Dad would beg me to talk to Patty. He knew she was going to run away. Patty would get on the phone. "They woke me up saying I was running away. I was sleeping." This happened many nights. Finally, Patty did run. Mother had another psychotic episode after Patty left, threatening to kill Mary and Larry. She tried to run them over with the car. Sharon came home. She and Bob drove the streets until by happenstance, or perhaps divine intervention, they spotted Patty walking along a sidewalk. They brought her home. Mother again was hospitalized.

Like Sharon, Mary had an adventurous, feisty personality. That, and her lack of coordination after the accident, helped her survive. Both Dad and Mom were more gentle with her, not entirely stopping punishment, but meting it out less often. When she was in high school, she began having seizures where she would blank out for a brief few seconds. Her school social worker discovered that her doctor had her on seven medications, several of them contraindicating each other. She put Mary in the hospital to help her go through withdrawal when a new doctor took her off all medications. The seizures ended. At the same time, Mother was on seventeen medications taken twice a day, prescribed by the same doctor. We'll never know what part those pills played in her psychosis, or her Alzheimer's.

I continued having Patty, and then Mary visit for the summer. Mother no longer resisted. These summers held many special memories. At the time, my husband and I lived next to a cemetery where one of the workers had tamed a robin so it would sit on his hand. I was as fascinated watching him as the kids were. As a frequent treat, I made brownies with marshmallows and a chocolate glaze. My kids along with Patty and Mary each got a tablespoon to scoop up warm gooey bites before the brownies completely cooled. Simple fun experiences helped create a home where they could enjoy being their wonderful selves. When Larry got older, Sharon took him home for the summer. He helped with her boat launching business and had good experiences with her and Bob and their three dogs.

One by one we grew into adulthood, each forging our way through remembered traumas to try to create a better life for ourselves and our own families. As Mary beautifully said, "You can either let the dysfunction destroy you or you can learn from it and make your life better." Each of us in our own way chose the latter.

While we sisters and brother had our disputes and differences, our sibling rivalry and angst, compared to the struggles we endured for our own and each other's survival, our differences diminished. We learned to accept those differences and grew to respect each others unique qualities. Perhaps in some strange way our struggles were a gift that brought us closer together in a strong bond of love and caring.

As an adult, I learned about the problems our parents had in their young lives. They themselves were products of dysfunctional families, Mom with her alcoholic father and Dad with a stepfather who wanted a wife but only begrudgingly accepted the child who went along with the marriage. Dad told me once that his stepfather never once spoke to him; instead, he carried on like Dad wasn't there. While this did not excuse the damage done to us, it made it understandable, and therefore forgivable. As an adult, I understood that they both wanted good for our family. The smoke from the dragons' fire of dysfunction made it impossible for them to see the way. In forgiving them I could show them the love and caring that they desperately wanted throughout their lives but didn't know how to get or give. It wasn't perfect, personalities didn't change, but edges softened.

Mother eventually joined a weekly recovery group which gave her enough emotional support that she needed no more hospitalization. When Dad became infirm and had macular degeneration, he was afraid we would get even for all he had done by putting him in a nursing home. Instead, he learned that we would love him and help him to live at home. We were alone in the living room one day when he asked, "Why are you doing this for me?" When I told him it was because I loved him, he shook his head and cried. Mother one day apologized to me. We were in her kitchen. "I am so sorry I couldn't protect you while you were growing up." She hugged me. In the ordinary days of family get-togethers and shared activities like playing cards, shopping, and going out for weekend breakfasts, we all began to heal. That healing opened a space for love.

Chapter 12

Who Is This Woman Named Barbara?

I spent a lifetime trying first to escape and later to move beyond the dysfunction that had shaped my life growing up. Little did I know that each step of that journey would bring me full circle in learning to forgive, love and care for my mother.

A pivotal experience between my childhood and adulthood was my years at the College of Saint Benedict, an all-girls Catholic college. The nuns were dynamic, well-educated women. My British literature instructor, with a degree from Oxford College in England, taught me to trust my analyzing while backing my assertions with facts. My German teacher, who spoke seventeen dialects fluently, taught me to love the language and culture of another country. My speech instructor, a woman who could have won awards in public theater for acting and directing, kept encouraging me to overcome my timidness until I was almost comfortable in front of a group. She also encouraged me to explore my creativity by dancing in and directing plays. Along with a rigorous education, all of us students were groomed to be self-motivated forces for good, whether in politics, business, or our families and neighborhoods. The nuns were our role models, active in national conventions, studying and traveling internationally, frequently incurring the wrath of the bishops in a conservative district for their controversial, modern actions at a time when the world was in the predawn era of the 1968 American upheaval.

I loved college. For the first time in my life I could decide how to style my hair, how to spend my time and money, and even what and how much to eat. While my class was notorious for the students' average twenty-five pound weight gain, I lost twenty pounds. The impact of the simple act of determining my nutrition desires and needs was profound. I was a free and independent woman, qualities I relished during the school year and reigned in when summers meant even harsher rules because my parents feared my new growth. I put up with summers knowing that I would soon be back at school.

I grew in many more personal ways. I learned the difference between being broke and being poor, though I couldn't have articulated it at the time. When my friends decided to throw away bars of soap and tubes of toothpaste that were near their end, I had them give them to me. They laughed and said that it was a good thing I wasn't rich, or I'd be a miser. However, using them saved me precious money. At the same time, I always found fifty cents to buy a flower for my room; gladiolus were my favorite because as the bottom florets died, new ones grew up the stems, my large flower growing ever smaller but still beautiful for several weeks. I bought a print of Van Gogh's *Starry Night* in the bookstore. Its deep emotions and blue beauty resonated with me. I graduated in May of 1964 with a major in English and minors in German, speech and drama, and education. I was ready to forge my own life.

While I admire people who create and carry out a plan for their lives, I mostly have gone galumphing through my own life, accepting what comes along and discovering new pathways as I go. When eventually I started my own family, I knew more concretely what I didn't want; I didn't want the tension I had felt growing up in my childhood home. I knew and felt what that was like. What I did want, joy and laughter, were vague concepts, dredged up from remembered moments my parents had given me. With a palette of colorful ideas and a blank canvas, I began to paint my dreams. Some were a mess; others were quite beautiful.

Joe and I married August 8, 1964, three months after my graduation from college. We were high school sweethearts. He had thick wavy black hair that always sported one errant curl which hung down on his forehead between two golden brown eyes. We both loved journalism, he with a camera, me with a pen. For one series, we interviewed local business leaders. I conducted the interviews while Joe took candid shots. We were a team. Weekly letters kept us together when college separated us physically. We became engaged my junior year in college.

I found a teaching job in Casselton, North Dakota, so Joe could finish his final three years of college to get a degree in pharmacy at North Dakota State University in Fargo. We rented a furnished basement apartment and soon became close friends with our landlord Don, his wife Audrey, and their four daughters, becoming godparents to their youngest daughter. Our next-door neighbors, wealthy farmers who frequently shared their beef with us at barbecues, also became good friends. On weekends we three couples often went to dances at the VFW club in town, the only bar the school board allowed me to frequent as a teacher. We also had several friends from campus, married couples who shared our circumstances. We had potlucks at one of our houses, played cards, and simply hung out together, all activities that required no money. In the fall, we ladies would walk through a woods scaring out deer for our husbands to shoot, our main meat supply.

I often wondered how such an unforgiving climate as that found in North Dakota could produce such warm-hearted people. Perhaps welcoming togetherness helped everyone survive the hot summers and bitter cold winters. I first experienced a *snirt* storm walking home from school one day, my hair and clothes dripping a combination of snow and dirt from surrounding fields. Then came the notorious three day blizzard in March of 1966, which brought Casselton to a halt. We watched the snow quickly cover our basement windows and then spent our days upstairs with our friends, combining our food supplies to create meals. We watched the snow creep up and cover their windows as well. At the end of the storm, Joe and Don had to shovel their way out of a garage window to get out of the house. Cars were buried; drifts covered the two-story house next door. Snow plows created roads wherever they could get through, including a vacant lot next to us.

March wasn't done with us. Three weeks after the storm, North Dakota hit record high temperatures. With the only trees along the river shading the snow and keeping the river frozen, the water from the snow that did melt formed a new river down our street. Throughout the night, Joe, Don and our neighbors sandbagged while Audrey and I went through our apartment, putting furniture on blocks and moving whatever we could to high shelves and tabletops. The next morning, while the men continued to sandbag, I, now five months pregnant, climbed up on a gigantic tractor from one of the large farms, the only transportation out of our area, and headed to school. I was late. While the principal unlocked my classroom door because I didn't have a key with me, he berated me for my tardiness. With the rest of the town going about its normal business, my story of flood, sandbagging and huge tractors sounded like a wild tale, like *the dog ate my homework*. I was too exhausted to try to explain, and I needed to get class started. I simply apologized.

Fifteen minutes into class the principal opened my door and motioned me over. "I just got a call. I am so sorry. I didn't know your street was flooding. The sandbags didn't stop the water from coming into your basement. They have two sump pumps going to keep the water as low as possible." He offered to let me go home for the day.

"There's nothing I can do there but watch the water come in. We've done everything we can to protect our things." I stayed to teach that day, my classes keeping me busy and distracted. I went home that afternoon to a water-free but muddy floor and a livable apartment.

Later that year, our son Louis was born on July 12, North Dakota's weather as wild in the summer as in the winter. We brought him home on a hot, windy day that blew dust through everything. I bundled Louis up for the 25-mile hot car ride home with the windows rolled up, carried him downstairs to our cool basement apartment, and took off all of his blankets. He survived.

Joe was in his final year of pharmacy school, driving the twenty-two miles each way. This was the year he had to dress professionally for all related classes, wearing either a lab jacket or white shirt and tie, all requiring starch and ironing, my least favorite chore. I continued teaching, walking Louis three blocks to the babysitters, an older couple who became like doting grandparents until the husband developed cancer. They kept Louis' bassinet between them during meals so they could admire him. She made a pink pillow with lace letters that said Little Louie, a name that could only be attributed to a Chicago thug, or our little brown-eyed, sandy-haired Louis. The name stuck with students and friends alike. One feeding time the spoon made a ping in his mouth, heralding his first tooth. We delighted in watching his first attempts at crawling. He would pull his legs up under him, put his head down on the floor, and shove backwards. He filled our lives with joy.

In 1967 Joe graduated and we moved to Brainerd, Minnesota, for his first job, managing Thrifty Drug Store and pharmacy. Louis spent his first birthday in a new home with his very own cake, chocolate frosting and all. He was a delight-ful chocolate mess. I got a job teaching tenth-grade English at Brainerd Senior High School. I was also pregnant again. The principal agreed to let me teach for half a year when I told him I wanted to experience a larger school system. An older lady who lived in the upstairs apartment of the house we rented, offered to watch Louis. She was perfect, even doing our laundry in her spare time.

Louis learned to climb that year. I'd find him standing on the counter reaching into upper cupboards. He'd climb up and down steps, always cautious enough to avoid falling. He also discovered the bottom cupboards. I had kettles and plastic bowls, which made perfect blocks and drums. His first walk in snow was more like a protractor drawing. He would lift one foot over and over, going in circles. The other foot was his stability, and he wasn't about to test what would happen if he ever lifted it. All the while, we were preparing him for his soon-to-arrive sister.

The semester ended the last week in January with surprise showers from all of my students. On February 15, 1968, eighteen months after Louis' birth, Christine was born at Saint Joseph's Hospital, just three blocks from our apartment. Where Louis slept through the night before he was one month old, Chrissey (she would create many versions of her name throughout her life) cried frequently for attention. I put her crib in the walk-in closet so our clothes could muffle her noise and let Joe sleep when he had to work the next morning. It made a perfect third bedroom. Her personality contrasted to Louis', much as Sharon's had to mine. As an infant, she would crawl off the bed or couch if we didn't watch her closely. When she started walking, she climbed the stairs and simply stepped off the top one, tumbling down, unlike Louis who would scoot down backwards on his hands and knees. At the lake, Louis played near the shore. Chrissey, on the other hand, walked off a close-to-shore drop-off. I dashed to save her. By the time I got back to the dock, she had walked off it again, fascinated by the way the ground just disappeared. At the pool, she would run to the diving board and jump in, not yet able to swim. I was thankful both children weren't so adventuresome. It was a full-time job keeping an eye on Chrissey.

When I got pregnant again, a two bedroom apartment wasn't going to hold all of us. We bought a house. The day we moved, Joe's assistant quit and Joe had to work a double shift. Our friends came and loaded a van with our belongings. When I caught them carrying out a sleeping Chrissey in her crib, I yelled "Stop!" and pulled her out. They figured she'd sleep the short distance to our new place. I knew better. I held her and Louis until it was time to leave our apartment. We once again were beginning a new phase of our lives with only a few months to prepare for a new baby.

On July 20, 1969, fifteen months after Chrissey's birth, Douglas was born. Maybe because he was my third child, I was more relaxed and enjoyed his time with me in the hospital. He was alert, looking at the lights and then back at me. He ate well when I nursed him the next morning. At noon however, he was fussy, refusing to eat. His cry seemed more like pain than distress. I held him up to my shoulder and rocked him until he relaxed. Joe came just before supper and promised to come back later. My parents were at our house, and he was going to make dinner for them. Shortly after Joe left, the nurse came to tell me Douglas was sick. They were having the doctor check him over. By nine that night he had died of a mass bacterial infection caught during his circumcision. The infection had attacked every organ in his body. "It spread like a dry brush fire," the doctor explained. Normally a gruff man with no bedside manner, he sat on a couch in the hall with me and cried. When Joe left at five, we were planning to bring a new little boy home the next day. At ten that night I held Joe and tried to soften the shock. The next morning I went home with only a baby book to hold on the car ride home.

When Joe and I got home, Dad and Mom hugged me and told me Chrissey was so sick they were ready to take her to the emergency room. Instead, I rocked her until she fell asleep in my arms. When she awoke she was better, perhaps having felt too deeply her brother's death. Louis also needed hugs but would quietly think about what his brother's death meant, needing hugs without words. He would talk about it later when he was ready. Mom fixed supper while Joe and I talked about burial plans. We then began the process of daily living that somehow continues even after a death.

I insisted on a full funeral, including a Catholic Mass. He may only have been a couple of days old, but he was my special little one. The funeral director provided a small white casket and services without charge, even though we didn't know him. Dad and Mom sat with us in the front of the church, all of us settling into the comforting familiarity of the service. Seeing two of our new friends sitting in the back of the church was also comforting, simply because they were there. I learned the comfort that comes from caring people, and that words don't matter if you just show up. We buried Douglas in the cemetery at the end of our block.

What surprised me during my grieving was a profound awareness of a loss of control over my life. In church, my empty arms ached when I heard a baby cry. When my children left the house to play or visit friends, I tried to rein in my panicky feeling that they would not come back, that something horrible would happen to take them from me too. I knew at a visceral level that the family canvas I had worked to create had been destroyed with one slash of a knife.

While Joe and I tried to comfort each other, my healing came with my having to help Louis and Chrissey understand what had happened. When, four months later, their paternal grandfather died, Louis was devastated. In a matter of less than half a year, we had moved from his neighborhood friends, another friend had moved to a different town, and two people close to him had died. By age three, he had experienced way too much loss. He was also my deep thinker. We would often sit around the dining room table, he and I talking about the deaths while Chrissey, only one and a half years old, listened.

"Is Grandpa in heaven with Douglas?" Louis asked. And later, "Will Grandpa get his leg back in heaven?" His leg had been amputated several years prior to his death. Another time, "Should we get Grandpa a car so he can get around in heaven?" We talked about each question, my assuring Louis that yes, Grandpa was with Douglas, he had his leg back, and he didn't even need a car to travel in heaven. Then came another question, "Am I going to die too?" I sucked in my own fear as I assured him that no, he was not going to die soon, that Douglas got very sick, unusually sick, that while we all die at some time, most often we were older, like Grandpa. Still, he had night terrors. We started talking to Grandpa and Douglas after bedtime prayers, just chatting, and it helped Louis to heal. His questions also helped me to heal. I had to talk about what Douglas' death meant. Through my children's eyes, I grew close to my infant child whom I now couldn't see but who was very much a part of our family.

Since we lived next to the cemetery, Douglas was close. Louis and Chrissey wanted to have lunch with their brother, so we would pack sandwiches and eat lunch by the grave. They would tell him about their adventures that day. In that way they learned to accept death as another dimension where, while they couldn't see their brother, he could see them. Chrissey should have been too young to really understand the deaths. Instead, I learned how deeply a toddler can comprehend difficult subjects when four years later, a kindergarten classmate rode her bike into the street and was killed. Several mothers called to ask if they could bring their children over. Chrissey had been telling them about her brother and how death led to heaven. She told them how they could talk to their friend. She shared a concept of death that helped her fellow students heal. Both she and Louis taught me how deeply young children can think. The language might be simple, but their understanding is profound.

Once the kids were in grade school, the cemetery became a playground. The neighborhood kids loved running through it as if it were a park. Part of it was built on a steep hill, perfect for charging bikes down the path and for skinning knees and elbows. Two rules were strictly ordered to be followed: you respect the graves, and you exit immediately when a funeral procession comes in. For the most part, they obeyed the rules, except for the one time Chrissey talked Louis into jumping into a freshly dug grave. The soil in the hole was too sandy to get a foothold to climb out. The grave was too deep to lower a bike for Louis to stand and hopefully reach the top. At first the kids were afraid to tell anyone; they knew they would be in big trouble with Mom. However, fear of an impending funeral and a casket over the hole, along with Louis' terrified pleas, finally convinced Chrissey to find a caretaker to free Louis. A trail of sand leading to a rocking chair in the living room and a teary-eyed Louis led to my discovering what had happened. When I threatened banishment from the cemetery, Louis assured me he would never try that again. I believed him. They continued to play and visit their brother in the cemetery for as long as we lived in that house.

Our home filled with fun lifelong memories, many of them around food. While I prepared the garden in the spring, Louis and Chrissey would jump and roll in the dirt, getting so dirty, I would hose them down before they entered the house. Later, they'd help me plant the vegetables and water them. In the fall, they loved to help me can tomatoes, peaches, and pears. Their favorite part was peeling the skin off the fruit. The canner would boil, bubble and steam, and soon we would have shelves of canned goods in the basement.

Both kids wanted to get merit badges in cooking, Louis for Scouts and Chrissey for Brownies. Theirs was no ordinary hamburger meal. Out of their *Look I Can Cook* book Louis planned a meal with baked fish and Waldorf salad. Chrissey chose chicken Kiev, refusing to touch the raw chicken, but pounding and filling each piece while I did the hands-on part.

One Thanksgiving we were unable to make our usual trip to celebrate with grandparents in Minneapolis. The kids were heartbroken. "Since we have to stay home," I suggested, "why don't you two plan and help cook the meal?" That year we feasted on fondued homemade corn dogs, Waldorf salad, and artichokes with hollandaise sauce. Dessert was pumpkin pie, because, the kids decided, we needed something traditional for our Thanksgiving meal!

Birthdays involved a cake of their choice from a book of designs and diagrams. I learned that frosting and coconut covered a multitude of mistakes. They were never works of art, but the kids loved them. Then came Louis' spaceship, big enough that it had to fit on the breadboard with the top hanging over. While we slept that night, ants discovered the part that hug over and crawled into the cake from the bottom. Off we went for a store-bought cake! The space-ship did a nose dive into the garbage can.

Joe had his own cake disaster. I had baked a cake for his brother's high school graduation and left it in the pans while I attended an AAUW (American Association of University Women) meeting. When I got home, Joe was holding a two-layer mound of cake pieces that even frosting couldn't fix. On top of the mound was a flag on a toothpick that said *Oh Shit*. I laughed, then he laughed, then we both sat on the floor, uncontrollably laughing. I baked another cake at his mother's house the morning of the graduation.

Not all memories involved food. When Louis was five and Chrissey three, we took them for an overnight canoe trip in the Boundary Waters. First we took them to a local lake and dumped them overboard, with life jackets on of course. That way they had a fun way of knowing what to do if the canoe should tip over during our trip. We paddled into the Boundary

Waters, stopped for a sandwich lunch, and set up camp on a rocky island. We built a fire, cooked supper, and had s'mores while the sun set. The kids roamed the small island freely, always in sight and always wearing life jackets. We got home with no incidents, except for a slight sunburn on the middle of Chrissey's back from her leaning over and exposing it when she fell asleep in the canoe.

Ordinary days were often filled with fun adventures. During storms, we would open the garage door, pull up lawn chairs, and watch the magnificent sight. More severe storms sent us to the picture window in the living room. Summers were spent at one of Brainerd's many lakes, swimming and playing with friends. Periodically, Patty and Mary would join us for a break from the tension Dad and Mom continued to create. Feeling adventurous one time, I successfully pierced Patty's ears with self piercers, hoops with a needle-like ends that we kept squeezing until they formed holes for the earrings I had bought her. I was less successful helping Mary learn to drive. When she drove forward instead of backing up, she swerved to miss the garage, drove across the lawn and finally found the brake moments before hitting the swing set. I suggested driver's training when she returned to school in the fall.

Winters, we skied, first cross-country, and then downhill. We cut down our tree each Christmas. After I made the mistake of reading the kids the story of *The Tree That Nobody Wanted*, we had years of trees so misshapen, we often had to screw a rope into the wall to keep them upright. One tree even had a bare spot that looked like a ski slope.

Louis was starting junior high school and Chrissey was in fifth grade when Joe got transferred to a new store in Blaine, Minnesota. A promised raise never came so I went back to teaching full-time to help with finances. Louis went from grade school, to a traditional junior high school, to an open concept school in a matter of months. Seventh grade was his time to act out. Then at the beginning of eighth grade, he told me, "I was pretty bad last year. I'm not going to be like that this year." And he wasn't. Chrissey was bussed to a distant grade school even though there were two schools within walking distance. Her teacher decided that she was a wild child because of her auburn kinky thick hair, so curly that it could only be combed when it was wet. What a contrast to her last three teachers in Brainerd who came to supper before we left and presented her with her first pair of pierced earrings. They had asked my permission first after they heard about her demand to pierce her ears or she wouldn't move.

When both kids eventually ended up at Northdale Junior High School at the same time, I was also assigned there. My job was to supervise a central learning center for students who were having trouble with their classes, those who had in-school detention, and special education students along with their assigned paraprofessionals. Louis thought this would be great fun. "We can walk to and from school together," he said. Many days we would skip and sing on our way home, arm in arm, laughing and sharing daily stories on what became neutral ground that turned the mother/son structure into a relationship of equals while we walked. Chrissey gave me a list of her rules, the first one being that teachers could only talk to me about her during conferences. I only broke that rule once. The assistant principal, a tough, no-nonsense man marched into my room early in the morning. "You have to come talk to your daughter. She came in late and when I scolded her she burst out sobbing. I can't get her to stop, and I can't handle tears." I found her in his office, still crying. Joe had yelled at her for being late when she left home. The principal scolding her was the final blow. I held her while we talked until she calmed down enough to go to class. Another time, during her eighth grade year, when she didn't know what to get me for my birthday, her science teacher suggested a star. Together they picked one out and she proudly pointed out which star was mine the night of my birthday.

By the time both kids were in high school, things started to fall apart at home. The support system I had developed in Brainerd was gone. While I started making new friends, I missed the ease of fitting into groups of longtime friends by myself when Joe worked nights and weekends. Upper management changed at Joe's company, making work less satisfying. My full-time teaching fulfilled me but left less at-home time. The tension I had worked so hard to sever from my life began, once again, to creep in.

While I thought I was handling everything fine, my body language spoke differently. Friends noticed the tension in my body and dark circles under my eyes. Over coffee, they told me how worried they were about me. While I assured them that I was OK, if not totally happy, their concern got me thinking. A week later, in my usual galumphing fashion, I drove past the turn to my house, drove to a counseling center, walked in, and said I was there to sign up for therapy with a licensed clinical psychologist for childhood abuse. I added that I didn't think my insurance would pay for anyone unlicensed.

Thus began years of therapy. When I first started, I thought of myself like a sponge, moist and supple with people's approval, dry and nonfunctioning with negative judgment or comments. If Joe told me a dress didn't look good on me, I never wore it again. If the kids argued or whined enough about a rule or consequence, I gave in. I was easily manipulated by anyone around me while I desperately tried to maintain the peace I saw slipping away. I also had a recurring dream of my standing in the middle of an empty oak wooden room. I slowly grew smaller and smaller until I simply disappeared. Through counseling, I gradually let go of past trauma and became more independently self-assured. The dreams stopped. My interactions with everyone around me shifted. As one friend put it, I was the same as I always had been, but I was totally different at the same time.

While I knew that when one person changes it upsets the rest of the family, especially the spouse, I was sure I could avoid the statistics. I was wrong. I was struggling to change, and Joe was struggling to keep us the same. The tension escalated. Then Chris (her high school name) got pregnant. We batted heads and forged out bottom lines. She insisted she keep her child. I insisted she live at home and finish high school. Louis became her advocate. He who was exceptionally bright and did not want to hurt his brain by studying, who was non-athletic and did not want to hurt his body, threatened anyone who made a comment about his sister, ready for any pain a fight might inflict. When my granddaughter Michele was born, I was glad I was teaching full-time. She was so adorable that I would have had a hard time keeping my mandate that Chris would be her mother, not me. I was supportive, but Chris was in charge. She was a wonderful mother. Throughout this time, I learned so much. Through our hashing out our differences, Chris and I grew to respect each other. Then, when my counseling created a more forceful mother, Louis and I also hashed out differences, which again led to respect.

One day Chris said to me "My friends are into such heavy drug use. They have really changed."

"No, honey. You have changed," I told her. "You are taking responsibility for Michele. You have really grown up this past year."

I learned that nothing is black and white. While I had a difficult time when Chris got pregnant, Michele proved to be a blessing. She gave Chris an excuse to say no to drugs. She brought joy into all of our lives after a tumultuous time. Only our little Michele could get Papa Joe to take his shoes and socks off and dangle his feet in the pool, the two of them side by side, just chatting and enjoying nature.

Throughout our difficulties, we still managed to have fun. We had family pool parties where adults and children played together. Louis baked his famous oatmeal bread for an elderly lady across the street, even after she called the police because she thought our mufflers were too loud. Together we grew and loved and came to a deep respect for each other as individuals. While my marriage didn't survive, the memories and the lessons we learned along the way have helped Joe and me maintain respect for each other.

"Life is what happens when you're making other plans," I have often told my children and my grandchildren. As a family, we continue to cut down our Christmas tree together and gather at my house where I make lunch while the adults put up my tree and put the lights on it. Then the kids add ornaments from the 1970s on, as high as they can reach, each year going a little higher. Watching them I realize that I didn't give up on my life's dreams. Instead, my personal canvas became a mural with all of us together painting our multicolored dreams and fears, tears and joys, a mural we called *family*.

As I helped my mother through her Alzheimers' journey, I realized how much I had learned from my family. When she could no longer communicate, my friends had taught me that words don't matter if you just show up. On the other hand, talking could help heal the pain of Mom's Alzheimer's for both of us, just as it had helped Louis and Chrissey heal their pain over losing their brother. I learned that just as we had related to Douglas at his grave, I could relate to Mother, even when it seemed like she had died as our mother and was replaced by a woman who was in many ways a stranger. When her mental capacity became that of a toddler and younger, I looked for the deeper thoughts and emotions beneath the muddled words. Most importantly, I learned that we all share interactions on many levels, giving and taking, loving and respecting, sometimes just hanging in there. These lessons and so many others were beautiful gifts from my family and friends that I could in turn regift to my mother, my lovely lady.

Chapter 13

Introduction to the Alzheimer's Ward

March 2010

It was the oldest part of the building, its aging structure a contrast to the pristine if drab building in which Mom's former room existed. The Alzheimer's ward looked like a worn out shadow of its earlier days. Still, there was a strange beauty that hinted of the way it stood when it was first built. It seemed to me to symbolize Mom's decline. Both showed the signs of their aging, both needed to be cared for, loved, and respected, more now than ever.

By 2010 we noticed another significant decline in Mom's cognitive ability. She was no longer capable of taking part in daily activities. She was regressing more and more beyond the care that the nurses and aides were trained to handle. The elevator system wasn't enough to keep Mom from wandering. Dr. Faber directed that Mom be moved to the Alzheimer's section of the building. The staff in the Alzheimer's unit were all trained specifically to take care of and interact with dementia patients. The activities were designed for each resident's fluctuating ability. A locked, coded door would assure Mom's safety. Reluctantly, we prepared to move Mom once again. The third floor had become another familiar place with familiar faces that we now had to leave behind.

The head nurse from third floor arranged to introduce us to the staff and show us Mom's room in the Alzheimer's ward before we moved her. We pushed a red button to get in while the nurse gave us the code to be able to leave. Sounds of moaning and yelling, people wandering aimlessly, so many unpleasant sensations assaulted us immediately when we entered the room. *I hate this place*, I thought. *It's like the worst movies about insane asylums. How dare Dr. Faber send her here. He won't even let her come home with us, and he's moving her to this strange place.* Outwardly, I smiled and kept talking with the nurse and my sisters.

When the nurse introduced us to the one who would be her counterpart, the Alzheimer's head nurse looked at us, smiled, and said, "So these are the famous sisters."

Surprised, I responded, "Are you sure you don't mean infamous?" I thought of our many demands and the way we watched over and advocated for Mom. We could be a royal pain.

"No," she said. "You take such good care of your mother and keep her room so homey and decorated. It's obvious how much you love her. Not many take such good care of our patients."

I was amazed, speechless. Everything we did seemed like the natural, only thing that we could do to make our mother's last days the best they could be. Didn't everyone do that? Apparently not as much as I thought. We proceeded to the end of one hallway. The last room on the right was Mom's. It was spacious with one wall mostly windows looking out to the parking lot and a park-like area of trees. It was much older, definitely not the Taj Mahal. Still, it would hold all the furniture from her other room and had wall space for her pictures. We would continue to pay extra for a private room. We would make this place home for Mom.

I reminded myself of my first impression of North Ridge and how that had changed because of the excellent care Mom received. I reminded myself of how wonderful and accurate Dr. Faber was. I would give this place a chance. If Mother could adapt to being here, so could I.

The more I visited Mom, the more those bizarre behaviors and vocalizations became unique, Alzheimer's-induced actions of lovable individuals. We came to know them as Mom's new family, the people she would spend more time with than with us. From the first time I visited Mom in the commons area of the Alzheimer's unit, I began to see all of the residents in a different light and met a few who would become regulars whenever I visited. Mom now preferred being out with the other residents and disliked being in her room. I wondered if its unfamiliarity made her feel less at home in her new place. Her old room was home to her, a place of refuge she recognized and could easily find when she returned from daily walks or the dining room. This room was older, and as much as we tried to duplicate her old one, it just was not the same. Still, she was content out here with the other residents.

She had her favorite chair, a green plush wingback that sat in a little space by the main desk, small and protected, yet part of the rest of the room. To her right she could watch the many-colored birds in the floor-to-ceiling glass cage. Straight ahead she could see the action in the dining area and walkways. She was like a queen looking over her subjects. We called the chair her throne.

On one early visit, we brought her new favorite treat, a chocolate frosty from Wendy's and pulled up chairs by her throne. The chaos and noise that had so bothered me at first had become a natural backdrop to our visits. While we sipped and ate the healthy Kashi cookies that Patty brought, we talked a bit. Then Mom drifted into her own world, telling stories of children, men who took her money, her protecting the children and telling the man to leave. This recurring theme had taken many variations: shopping, taking neighborhood kids on outings, protecting her house from unscrupulous people, again almost always men. I thought of the time she apologized for not being able to protect me from Dad. I thought of the time she told Dad that I was old enough to be getting my period, that his spankings could harm my reproductive organs. She had found a way then to stop the beatings without having repercussions of her own. Now she was unemotional during her stories, droning on until my attention drifted. I started listening to what was going on around us.

One man loudly yelled, "They'll never know." A lady in another part of the room responded, "Oh yes they will. They already know." The man repeated, "They'll never know," to which she again repeated the same words, a word bantering that was like a distorted conversation. Another lady walked by, her rambling reminding me of the way Mother walked in her own world, talking to herself. "It's OK if I can't come see you tomorrow," she muttered. "I love you." She walked into a locked entryway which served as a sun room on this bright, yet chilly spring day. Soon she was talking to the windows, staring vacantly, like the window was more a wall and the outdoors non-dimensional. While I watched the woman, another woman, whom we lovingly named the *stealth thief*, pushed her wheelchair towards us, saying, "I can't see it." She closed in and grabbed two cookies. Patty just laughed. Mom glared at her.

"That's the woman who took Mom's doll," Patty informed me. "Mom was furious, but I told her she'd bring it back; and she did."

The woman walked her wheelchair into the sunroom, eating her cookies. Later, she returned holding a soft, stuffed bear. Mom held her Easter lamb, looked at her, and smiled, the two sharing some commonality, some positive emotion, Mom's past anger gone. Then the woman put her bear on Mom's walker and maneuvered her walker away. Before she left, she went for the cookies again, looked at them, and put them back.

"I guess she doesn't like your healthy cookies," I teased Patty.

A man wheeled himself out, yelling, "They want my pee. I can't do it. I can't give it to them."

One of the aides tried to comfort him, telling him that it was OK. He didn't have to give it to them now. On his tray sat a plastic container for him to urinate into. The aide put on a rubber glove and took the container.

"I can't pee," he kept yelling.

"I'll put this by your bed so you have it when you want it," she assured him. She left with the container. As soon as it was out of sight, he calmed down.

I thought of the times when Mom talked about people telling her what to do, to leave her room, to go places or do activities. I knew the staff would bring her down for activities, for meals, for snacks and singing. To her they were being bossy, even if they were gentle, and even if she wanted to be where they took her. It reminded me of a toddler in the terrible twos, asserting nos and negative emotions while they explore new boundaries, only now it was in reverse.

Having finished her frosty, Mom noticed mine sitting on the ledge of her walker, for now our table. She took it and started to drink it. When she got to the bottom of the cup, she started taking it apart, making a mess with her straw and almost dropping the cup. I instinctively reached out to grab the cap and straw. Mom glared at me, grabbed onto her things, and looked like she was ready to hit me.

Patty intervened, softly telling Mom, "Let me hold these for you," while she slowly took the top and straw, and handed her a spoon to get at the bottom. Mom cooperated with her without hesitation. The suddenness of my moves set up a protective emotion in Mom, again reminding me of a young child. Her defensive mood gone, she happily finished my chocolate cooler.

When Mom complained of being cold, I wrapped my coat around her, noticing a cough that I hoped wasn't the start of a cold. I was glad I didn't come to see her last Sunday when I was in the midst of a sniffling, coughing cold. One less thing to feel guilty about. The last thing I wanted to be responsible for was her feeling miserably sick when, again like a young child, she wouldn't understand what was happening to her. "Does that feel better?" I asked her. She smiled, nodded *yes*, and was soon in a deep sleep.

While Mom slept, another woman whom we dubbed Ella from Alma approached and sat on the one empty chair by us. "Isn't it a nice day?" she asked. "I'm from Alma, Wisconsin." While we chatted about the weather, I was amazed at her clarity and ability to carry on at least some semblance of a conversation. She seemed like she didn't belong here, but perhaps she was midway through her Alzheimer's journey; perhaps she was here because she wandered. She was still a sharp contrast to the rest of the muttering, yelling, and discordant interactions. I handed her the bear that the other woman had left on Mom's walker. She petted it and then cuddled its softness to her, smiling. How constant was the need to touch, to hug something soft. For Mom, her dolls and animals became her children, at times her companions, always as real and alive to her as we were, often more present to her, even when we sat next to her. She would talk to us, and then she'd be gone into that world we didn't share or understand, talking to her animal and listening to what the animal said back to her, a conversation beyond what we could comprehend.

A volunteer began playing the piano. "'Blue Moon'" I said, "From *Breakfast at Tiffany's* with Audrey Hepburn." Only those who knew me knew how amazing this recollection was. I seldom remembered titles of movies or the names of the stars in them. "I love this song," I continued.

"Me too," said the woman, still holding the bear. Patty rubbed Mom's arm, in part to wake her so she could enjoy the music. Mom was in a deep sleep. She didn't even respond when

I pulled my coat from around her shoulders. We left, knowing that when Mom woke up, she wouldn't have any awareness of our having been there. I once again consoled myself in thinking that our interactions with her and the treats we brought positively affected her emotionally, making her day more pleasant. At some sensory level, she knew she was loved. At least, that was my hope when I keyed in the code to leave and walked into the now warm spring air, chatting with Patty as though this was an ordinary day, our lives out here as disconnected from Mom's world in there as hers was from ours. We continued our separate journeys through another week.

Chapter 14

Stories from Mom's Alzheimer's Home and Family

2010–2013

Have you ever averted your eyes at the sight of a homeless person, or imagined the strange place he or she calls home? What would happen if you got to know each individual person? How would that shift your impressions? That is what happened as I got to know Mom's new family, with all their bizarre behaviors and unique personalities. I came to enjoy each person and looked forward to seeing all of them on my visits..

Visiting Mom during lunch always provided some new experience. One time, Mom was sitting at a table with three other people, staring at half of a hot dog like she wasn't sure what it was. The other half was on the floor. After kissing her *hello* and having her taste the strawberry-banana smoothie we brought, Patty cut up her food and began feeding her.

While Mom ate, we talked and laughed, Patty and I never quite sure what the conversation was about or where it was going. It was funny how normal these conversations had become. Mom often pointed out people and happenings around us which only she could see. She muttered gibberish about them; we pretended we knew what she was saying and made some comment, and then we watched them leave, as though they were really there. Other times she went into her stories, going on and on, while we picked out bits and pieces. Mom connected to us with eye contact, laughed, punched me in the arm when she misunderstood something I said, and then with a twinkle in her eye forgave me.

Across the table from us, a woman watched our interaction, eating bits of food. Trying to get the attention of an aide, she motioned repeatedly for them to come over. When that didn't work, she started yelling "Help!" over and over again. We had often heard her going on like this for long periods of time. It always seemed like this was her Alzheimer's babbling. Now, we saw her desire for attention. Nobody paid any attention to her. Suddenly, she started rocking the table violently. Milk, coffee, juice and food splattered everywhere. Patty and I grabbed the table to lessen the effects of her *tantrum*. While the aides only noticed her acting out, we saw her escalating her demand to be noticed until people could not help but pay attention to her. I thought about a time when I was on an airplane watching an infant go more and more into a rage because he did not like the pressure of taking off. Only when his mother fed him did he quiet down. Whatever her mental age, the woman knew how to finally get the attention she craved with people rushing from all directions to quiet her.

Patty and I chuckled as we watched the commotion, helped clean up the spills, and helped Mother finish her dessert and smoothie. Then we took Mom back to her room for a nap. Kissing her and promising to return, we left her holding her baby doll and telling it sing-songy stories as she drifted into sleep. "That was something else again," Patty said. I pushed the magic number code to let us out. "It sure was," I chuckled. "If nothing else, it certainly isn't dull when we visit."

On my way home from visiting Mom one day, I was listening to Garrison Keillor. He started his Lake Wobegon story, telling of the need for a new pastor for the Lutheran Church in town. While he wove his tale of the search for a new minister, switching to a cafe in another town where the waitress had decided to answer the call to the ministry, on to a town dog who loved blueberries, roaming randomly from subject to subject, I found myself getting agitated by his ramblings. It sounded way too close to Mom's chanting stories that I had just left. What, I wondered, is the fine line behind stream-of-consciousness stories that propel a man to fame and fortune, and the stories that Mom told in her dementia? His subject was the life of a make-believe town. Hers was a composite of her earlier life and make-believe. Both told tales of people in their periphery. The similarity was uncanny, haunting.

Patty and I had brought Mom her usual Caribou smoothie today, this flavor, pomamango. She took a napkin and then asked for another. Running her fingers over the decorative blue lines on the white napkin, she began reading as if the napkin were a storybook. She told of children coming in and out of the house; of men who wanted to come to her party, and her not letting them in because they wouldn't pay; she talked about living in Robbinsdale as a child and later as an adult. On and on she chanted her story while she traced the lines on the napkins. Occasionally, she would pause, stare at the line as though trying to figure out a word, stumble a bit over its pronunciation, and then smiling, proud of herself, pronounce the imagined word and continue her story. When she got to the bottom of the napkin, she lifted it up and continued reading the second napkin. After she reached the bottom of the second series of lines, she looked up at us, smiled, and was once again aware of us.

It was not a good day for her being present with us. After her storytelling, she began talking to her doll, carrying on a conversation during which it was obvious that she heard the doll talking back to her. She would ask it if it were tired, if it wanted to play. *You want a toy? Maybe after your nap.* The words weren't clear, but close enough for us to get the gist of the conversation. More and more she lived in her own world when we were with her. Gentle touches, offering her a drink of her smoothie, bringing her treats to eat, all brought her back less and less. We'd have short periods of interactions, talking about the people around her, and while I often had no clue what she was really saying, at least it was some semblance of communication.

So often I had cried, feeling guilty because she didn't want me to go. Now, she was barely aware I had been there once I was a mere few feet away. This leaving was in some ways easier, but also more disturbing. I used to say that by the time I hit the interstate, she no longer remembered I was there. Now I was gone from her before I left the room. When I first came today, she looked at me with that vacant stare I have come to recognize all too well. "Who are you?" she asked. I smiled, bent down to kiss her and said, "I'm Barbara, your favorite daughter." Patty vehemently shook her head *no*, and we all laughed. I'm not sure she even really knew me or Patty as her daughters, but perhaps our decades-long fun bantering about *Mom likes me best* among us four girls stuck somewhere in her memory. Whatever else, we were connecting, we were laughing, and Mom was happy. I still hoped and maintained that the emotional affect of happiness and laughter remained with her, even when the concrete memory of us vanished. Maybe the following week I'd enjoy Garrison more. Now I turned him off and put in a CD.

I don't know why I sang that particular song one day when I visited Mom. We were out in the entryway where the fall colors and sunshine could lift my spirits and hopefully Mom's. Out of the blue, I started singing *You Are My Sunshine*. Mom's eyes lit up and soon she was singing along with me. Some words were her own, some recognizable, but the melody was ours together.

The next day I heard on the radio that the number one song used in hospice care was, *You Are My Sunshine*, used to lift the mood of the patients. Serendipity struck again! I began to sing it every time I visited Mom. One time, we sang in chorus, our eyes looking closely at each other, joy flowing between us. So often in the past Mom had been disconnected, unable to interact with me. Now, we sang, eye to eye, a sparkle passing between us while we sang. Once again, this disease, which had taken so much away, gave us a pure moment of expressed mutual joy.

The following Easter, I found a plush yellow duck that sang *You Are My Sunshine* when you squeezed its orange webbed foot. It added a new dimension which delighted Mom. Then one day we played it in the commons area with Mom. Soon most of the residents were noisily singing with us, a former drummer pounding the table in rhythm to the tune. After a few fun times, the duck disappeared. We were used to traveling items and discretely checked the residents' rooms. No duck. When we had our next staff meeting, I suggested to them that they stole the duck because of the commotion it caused. No one admitted to it, but no-one denied it either. We continued to sing without its accompaniment, a few close-by residents joining in. Long live the sunshine song!

A news headline linking five new genes to Alzheimer's caught my attention in the *Star Tribune*. While these genes could be a slight indicator, one earlier discovered gene, APOE, a cholesterol metabolism gene, is said to increase the likelihood of Alzheimer's 400% if one parent has the gene and 1,000% if both parents have the gene (Gina Kolate; "5 new genes linked to Alzheimer's identified"; *Star Tribune*; April 4, 2011).

"I beg to differ," I thought to myself. "That isn't the case in my family. Your evidence doesn't always ring true."

Dad was the one who had high cholesterol in our family. His mind was sharp right up to the day a massive heart attack killed him before he even hit the ground. On the other hand, Mom had good cholesterol, but high blood pressure. She was the one whose mind slowly deteriorated, the one who now lived in a world that we couldn't grasp and could only share on her good days. My experience opposed Dr. Michael Boehnke's assertion of strong evidence for the gene's relation to Alzheimer's.

My stake in the doctor being less than right was personal. My dad's cholesterol was hereditary. I struggled to keep mine below 250. Most medications demolished my muscles, leaving my wrists in pain and causing my legs to spasm with enough pain to wake me several times a night. "I won't trade possible future hell for the hell I endure with these statin drugs," I defiantly stated to a doctor who tried to scare me into continuing them by recounting the devastation that can occur with a stroke. "Beside, I'm a dancer, and I want to continue dancing at least into my 70s, not be debilitated from drugs." Alzheimer's added another layer of concern. In her forties, my daughter was beginning to see her cholesterol also rise, even though she was a fit personal trainer and nutritionist. While I had adjusted to my mother's Alzheimer's, I didn't want to live with such a disease. I put the newspaper away, one more piece of information on Mom's disease, one more attempt to fit together the mysterious pieces of this Alzheimer's puzzle.

On visiting days when Mom had some memory and clarity, I wondered what it would be like if a method of reversing the disease, or rerouting the memory paths could happen. I had become so accustomed to Mom in her present condition that it seemed to now be an integral part of her. I would once again have to relearn who my mother is. It would be a huge transition, much better than the death of her creative, productive self, but still another leap into a new Mom. The positive reward would be a world of more lunches and fun times together, of marveling at her renewed creativity in sewing and crafts.

Now her hands moved in memory of those days, even while her mind couldn't keep up with her body's memory. "I made this," she'd tell me, her hands moving over a necklace, her doll, or her own blouse.

"You did such a wonderful job," I'd reply, my memories of a green velvet coat with fur collar, dolls and clothes made for me and later my children, cross-stitching, crocheted blankets, and so much more filling my heart along with my memory. Perhaps, somewhere in her deteriorating mind some semblance of similar memories remained. We smiled, and I touched her hand while she gently stroked pretend creations.

The previous night when Mary and Candace, her daughter, went to see Mom, an aide was wheeling her back to her room. It was a startling sight. Mom had always been mobile, using her walker for stability, when she remembered and didn't leave it somewhere. The aide explained that they had been using a wheelchair at night when Mom was tired and less stable on her feet. She assured Mary that Mom was still walking everywhere during the day. Still, it was one more little sign of her regression. Mary and I talked about how Mom slept more now, a progression of her disease. Mary was OK when she talked to me, but I could tell the incident had shaken her.

"She was so tired, so I just held her hand and stroked it," Mary told me.

"Patty and I have the advantage of coming during the day when she is more alert," I told her. "I've started playing ball with her again, and she does quite well."

Determined to help Mom relearn some basic skills, Candace had her sing the alphabet with her and do her numbers. Because it was Candace, Mom did her best, but most often couldn't follow along. Still, Mom worked with Candace on those skills where she would become agitated with the rest of us. I think it was Candace's thirteen-year-old spritely manner. On another night, Candace commented on how pretty Mom's nails looked. "What color are they?" she asked.

Mom looked her in the eye and said, "Are you testing me?" Just a brief moment of clarity.

It reminded me of a previous time when Mary and Candace were visiting. Candace was trying to cajole her mother into getting some goodies at the grocery store after they left Mom. "I am too exhausted; you'll have to wait until tomorrow," Mary told her. When further pleadings ended in definitive nos, Candace began making faces at Mary to show her disgust at not getting her way.

Mom looked directly at Candace. "You and Barbara and your evil ways," she blurted out.

Mary laughed when she told me. I feigned total shock. "I wasn't even there!" I said. Mom hadn't recognized me, except on one or two rare occasions, for two years or more. Incidents like this made me wonder where Mom's momentary commentaries, her moments of clarity came from. I thought of all the times when Mom misinterpreted what I said, hearing totally different words. "What did you say?" she'd ask and punch me in the arm. "I'm going to have an indented left arm from her punching me," I jokingly told everyone. In reality, the punches were light, almost playful, followed by our touching foreheads, my asking her if she was mad at me, her smiling and our both laughing, communication at a most basic, physical level.

However, from some past emotion or experience, perhaps from when I started doing sweat lodge ceremonies and fire ceremonies, Mom had a deep-seated memory of dislike about my choices in life. Ours had long been a complex relationship, with a lot of healing occurring during Mom's later years. Perhaps, I decided, I should quit being my cat-worrying self and just laugh at the humor of Mom's moment of clarity, wherever in her brain it came from.

I went to see Mom alone one day, Patty saying she'd come a bit later after running errands. I was always amazed that Patty could spot Mom from across the room. At first, to me many of the patients looked just like her. I finally spotted her at the end of the dining room, an aide helping her eat lunch.

"I'll take over for you," I said. The aide introduced me to make the transition easier, then handed me the fork and left.

"How are you doing today, Geri?" I asked. Using her name still, after all these years, seemed disrespectful, but the nurses and social worker said she preferred to be called *Geri*, and so I took one more step in letting go of my mother.

While I fed her, I noticed that she was less capable of doing it herself. It had been a month or so since I was there during a meal, choosing to go mid-afternoon to fill in her alone time. I took the rind off the ham, making it easier for her to chew, blended it with sweet potatoes, and gave her sips of the Caribou Snowdrift I had brought her to wash it down. She giggled when I snuck a bite of her cake to determine that the yellow rivers running through the white cake were indeed lemon, one of her lifetime favorite dessert flavors. She took the fork from me and tried to eat the cake herself, but she couldn't quite make it work, even when I cut the cake into bite size pieces for her. It pained me to watch her struggle with the fork, and later a spoon, unable to get only a few crumbs to her mouth. She gave me the fork, and I finished feeding her. Mom's steps into this disease seemed infinitesimally small now, baby steps into her regression. I was surprised and thankful that among all those in wheelchairs, Mom still walked, though I noticed she had more trouble getting out of chairs, her legs wobbly as she struggled to find her first few steps. Once in motion, she kept going where we directed her or on her own to one of her favorite chairs.

While we were eating, another woman at the table, Alma, wanted some of my attention, too. She talked about being from Wisconsin, about how she liked the cake, too. When I moved her plate so she could more easily get at her cake, she smiled and said "Thank you." Last week I had met her daughter when they were walking by where Mom sat with Patty and me. Alma looked at me and said, "I think I'll go for a walk." Her daughter was coaxing her to move, so I said, "That's a good idea. You go walk. I'll be right here when you get back." "OK dear," she said and off they went. This day Alma had several greeting cards. She ran her fingers over one and read, wife. I'd almost forgotten there was a time when Mom could read words, her favorite being a book about the Pope. She'd read some words and then go off into story about the Pope asking her to help him after she met him. Alma simply said, *wife* and started sobbing. Suddenly her expression changed. "No!" she said, stopping the tears with with a fiery look in her eyes and a tightening of her facial muscles. She looked at me. "I'm sorry," she said. I told her that it was OK to cry, that sometimes tears helped us. At the same time, I fed Mom and talked to her, noticing that she got crabby when I paid attention to someone else.

Later, Patty came with two of her grandkids, and we moved to the sunroom where we could look outside. I pointed out the freshly planted flowers to Mom and listened to her stories, nodding my head or adding comments, picking out a few words in the ramblings. When Patty and I talked about our week, I noticed that Mom didn't like the attention drifting away from her, so I turned back to her and started singing our favorite song, *You Are My Sunshine*. She joined in halfheartedly this time, unlike the spirited times previously. Then she went back into storytelling mode.

When we got ready to leave, she became angry, pursing her mouth to ward off goodbye kisses. At this point, I should have been immune to this gesture, yet it brought back painful memories of growing up with a mother who battled depression and mental illness, who manipulated us children by the love she withheld when she was angry with us. I felt a familiar sting in my heart. Patty started to leave, but I told her that I would stay a bit longer to try to help Mom through this anger.

Mom talked about a man who was gone, who was sick, who left her and didn't return for forever. I couldn't tell whether she was talking about her dad, who was a violent drunk, or her husband, who left her with me as an infant during World War II. Whichever, she was feeling lost, abandoned. We talked a few minutes, the mood passed, and she started talking to her baby doll. She soon was much better than before, her anger forgotten. I was the one left with a heavy heart, knowing that even this disease couldn't erase all of the symptoms of her depression. Her loving openness to everyone now was who she had become without the pain of her past. Yet, every once in a while that past reared its ugly head to bite her, and me. I reminded myself that it's all about Mom, about making her days as positive, gentle, and happy as possible. I flicked a speck of hurt off my heart, caught up with Patty, and we left for a barbecue at Mary's house.

Once again, I arrived to visit Mom before Patty. I dreaded this alone time, with no partner to take up slack spaces in our inter-actions. On the other hand, I looked forward to time with just Mom and me. I found her sitting in one of the chairs placed along the hall for those who needed to rest during their walks.

"Hi, lovely lady," I greeted her, kissing her forehead. She looked at me with that initial blank stare, then smiled a garbled greeting. "Let's go to your room today," I suggested. I tried to coax her to her feet; then, using the method I observed with the caretakers, I took both of her hands and gently pulled her forward and up. It worked. I transferred her hands from mine to her walker handles. Then we walked ever so slowly down the hall.

Once in her room, I tried to get her to sit down, but she resisted moving toward her chair. Instead, she started humming and swaying. She put her arms around me and soon we were dancing together. Mom swayed her hips, joyously, sensuously.

At first, I stiffly braced myself to be ready to catch her in case she lost her balance. A fall could be deadly. Soon, though, I relaxed and simply followed her lead, humming whatever arose from within and dancing to our own freestyle rhythm. When I finally directed her to her chair, she turned and hugged me, a great big bear hug. We stood embraced for several minutes.

"Thanks," Mom said. "That feels good to me." Her words were clear, not the usual mix of unintelligible sounds and muddied language I had come to accept.

"It feels good to me, too," I told her. We both smiled as she sat down. I thought about early dance lessons that Mom took me to and the many times she came to my adult performances with my sisters. I wondered how much she would have liked to have danced when she was younger, how much she relived those desires through my dancing.

While Mom watched from her chair, I started taking the Christmas decals off the window and putting the other decorations on the bed to take home. I began talking about my week, lunching with the grandkids, dance class, general chit-chat. Mom smiled and nodded, probably not understanding much of what I said. She looked relaxed, a smile on her face and a starry twinkle in her blue eyes. I squeezed the hand of the snowman-and-dog toy on her table, the one that sang *Jingle Bells*. While the snowman sang, the dog barked out the music. Mom bounced her body, humming and singing a few words that she could remember. At the end of the song, the snowman belted out a long-held *way!* while the dog, and I, howled, *awoo!* Mom laughed delightedly and motioned for me to play it again. I went around the room singing, howling, and taking down decorations.

None too soon, Patty walked in with Mom's smoothie and my iced tea. There are only so many times one can howl out "Jingle Bells" and stay relatively sane. Mom drank some of her smoothie; then she took her straw out, splashing liquid everywhere. Patty put the straw back and encouraged Mom to finish drinking.

"It's past Valentine's Day," Patty laughed while I hung heart-shaped garlands around Mom's pictures.

"I know. I got this at half price. Mom doesn't know the difference, and it will keep her room festive looking," I answered. Mom thoroughly enjoyed the dazzle and color of decorations whenever they were up. She was time and holiday oblivious.

When Mom dozed off, we gathered the Christmas decorations, leaving the snowman. We kissed her *goodbye*, and left. She didn't stir, didn't know we were leaving, and wouldn't remember we were there when she awakened. I still believed she would be happier for the rest of the day, even though she wouldn't know or care why.

Back home, I thought about what was lost and what was gained with this bizarre disease. Throughout my life, numerous times I had tried to kiss Mom *hello* or *goodbye*, touching lips drawn in a tight line across her face to prevent any interaction. Along with all the good that Alzheimer's took away from Mom, it also took away her phobias, her fears, the mental illness and the depression that had plagued her throughout her life. That stripped away, we could share a long hug and closeness, beyond what we could have had without her Alzheimer's. Still, I missed our many lunches at Thistle's in Robbinsdale during the early stages of her dementia. I missed the after-lunch trips to the flower shop just a half block away. I missed the countless hours spent tying blankets for relatives, friends, and the church baby center for disadvantaged mothers. For a brief moment, I wiped away tears about what had been lost, but then I smiled at the beautiful day we had just spent. Today we danced!

Chapter 15

My Love of Dance

It was afternoon, the sun shining on the golden dance floor of Ascension School gym. I was three, learning my first brush, brush step. How could I imagine at that young age that dance would be my expression when I was vocally silenced, that I would one day dance with birds and join a worldwide dance movement for clean water; that dance would connect me to my mother like words never could?

It was lifelong. I felt like my arms were chained to my sides, my body stiff, ready to protect myself, afraid to be my exuberant self. When I danced, I broke those chains and let the joy flow out of me.

I often wonder if my one dance with Mom fulfilled a deep desire in her to enjoy the freedom of movement that dance gave me throughout my life. I wonder if she started me with lessons to give me what she didn't have or to live vicariously through me. Perhaps she brought me to dance; perhaps it was my grandmother, her mother, who often took over my care to help Mom out. All I know is that I fell in love with dance from the first sound of my tap shoes, a love that would last a lifetime.

I now work at the front desk of a dance studio, which adds another dimension to my love of dance. Along with performing a multitude of tasks as the go-to person at the front desk, I also share the joy of the students and lighthearted conversations of their parents. Young siblings play in a toy kitchen area or read the books stacked in one corner. The feel of a huge, noisy family shifts to a quiet few parents who stay for the late evening classes of the older students.

I have particularly enjoyed working on cold winter nights when I traded my *now it's dark, let's sit and turn on the TV* for meaningful work and social interaction. The dance assistants, a group of teenage young ladies who help teach classes and perform assigned chores have become like my adopted family. I started signing their work slips by making smiley faces out of my initials, the challenge becoming to create new ones for each season. At the beginning of one year, I made mint brownies for them with a note that said, *Have a sweet, fun year of dance.* Now it's a tradition, along with other sweets throughout the year. On Thursdays, my day ends with an adult clogging class. We are a bit rowdy, always fun-loving, and cheer each other on with new difficult steps with our motto, *Close enough to perfect for us.*

The sounds of the youngest students stomping their tap shoes the minute they walk through the studio door onto the wood floor brings back memories of my first dance classes. Just like these youngsters, I gradually learned to control my body movements to perform the steps. I can still hear my *brush brush step*, two softer sounds followed by a *loud-as-I-could-make-it stomp* keeping rhythm.

I fell in love with dancing as a toddler in 1945 at Dorothy Lundstrom's School of Dance in North Minneapolis. She'd roll a piano into the Ascension School gym on which her nephew played the songs to which we danced. Jazz proved more difficult for my round, little body. I never got my legs to touch the floor when I tried to do the splits. Dorothy would gently push me down, ever so slowly until I almost succeeded. The minute she let go of my shoulders, up I would pop, my legs forming an arch instead of a split! Forward and back rolls were more abstract movement than anything else. Dorothy lovingly called me her little cupcake.

Dorothy had connections to New York. The success of her older students in getting on stage in the "Big City" fueled my melodramatic imagination. I would croon "On Top of Old Smokey" and other songs, dancing along the sidewalk in front of my house. Dorothy also had modeling connections. Once I entered grade school, I took modeling along with dance. I still remember the runway walk: toe down first, then heel, tall straight body. Balancing a book on our heads assured perfect posture while we strutted across the room.

Taking modern dance in college turned me from someone who enjoyed dancing into a dancer. I donned a black leotard and tights and learned dance as a time-space art form. When I started creating my own dances, the music flowed through me, dance becoming as much a part of me as the blood flowing through my veins. My body expressed my deepest emotions, both intense and humorous. For our final project senior year, my best friend Ann and I choreographed a dance together to *Exodus*, the theme song from the movie about the Jews move to Israel in 1948. Our tight, trudging steps slowly evolved into circular swirls of jubilation, symbolizing the joy of finally finding a home. I had studied the plight of the Jews in my world history class. Through my dance, I empathized with their experience in a way I never could have done in a class.

After college, beginning a new marriage, a new teaching career, and eventually birthing a new baby boy left no time to even consider formal dance classes. Still, my body insisted on moving to music. On weekends I would play lively tunes and dance around the house while I cleaned. Dusting was magically transformed when it began with a pirouette and ended with a sweep of the dust cloth across a wood surface.

I have found over the years that impromptu dancing can lead to interesting experiences. In my now home on a golf course and wetlands in Saint Francis, Minnesota, I have a bird feeder where I can enjoy wildlife such as birds and deer and fox from my sunroom windows. One day while cleaning, I heard a song for dog food on a television commercial. I danced into the sunroom singing *Baby I'm Worth It* along with the ad, flailing my arms exuberantly. When I looked out the window, two cranes danced around each other beneath my feeder, watching me while I watched them. To this day, when I see the cranes, I bring food to the feeder, we dance, they move back a few feet and then come to eat while I am still spreading their food.

At other times spontaneous dance can be embarrassing. One day recently when I was shopping with Patty at Penney's, she suddenly looked at me with fear clearly evident in her eyes. "We need to go now," she said. "I need to go to the emergency room." Her blood pressure had suddenly dropped dangerously low, a chronic health problem for her. Once there, the doctor ordered an intravenous drip to stabilize her system.

While we waited for it to take effect, I decided to act goofy to brighten her mood and relax her. I went to the foot of her bed and began dancing and singing *Let Me Entertain You.* Soon we were both laughing. Then she said, "Barb, look over your right shoulder." I hadn't noticed that the ER was circular, built around a central staff area with windows toward the center for easy patient monitoring. Four laughing faces looked back at me. When the doctor came back into the room he told Patty she was stable enough to go home. Then he looked at me. "You, we're not sure about yet," he laughed.

When I moved to Brainerd, Minnesota, in 1967, the school district's community education program offered belly dancing for credit. I immediately signed up. I made a blue chiffon skirt and dance bra, bought finger cymbals, and headed to class where women of all shapes, sizes, and ages gathered for a fun new experience. After learning several moves, we put them together into a dance. I still have a picture of my diverse class performing our recital in the technical school hallway. A background poster selling flowers announced, *Roses: Last Chance.* I laughed then at the irony and still laugh when I see the picture today. As an added bonus I received renewal licensure units for the class because it was offered through the school district, and because I had speech and drama certification. I just might be the only teacher in Minnesota who advanced her teaching career through belly dancing!

I began taking regular tap and jazz dance classes in 1979 after our move to Coon Rapids where a good friend had recently opened a dance studio. Eventually, my daughter also took tap lessons with me and later became a dance assistant. My dance album records our years of performing together, starting with tap dancing and progressing to clogging. A favorite picture shows us in red sequined costumes with black fringe, holding the cane we used to tap to *New York New York*.

When my friend's daughter took over the studio, she added clogging and a mother/dancer component to the year end gala. By this time, my granddaughter Michele was also dancing. I now clogged monthly in a performing adult group, but the highlight of each year was dancing at the year-end show with our three generations. Christine was always calm and confident before performances. Michele and I were nervous and edgy. Likewise, Christine became the lead person in our trio, the one we looked to when unsure of ourselves. The one time she blanked on part of the dance, we all momentarily fell apart. While we finished the dance in fine style, Michele was furious, vowing never to dance with us again. Of course, that was embarrassment talking. We would have many fun future dances together.

Once granddaughter Michele was in high school, she also became a dance assistant at the studio. At the end of her senior year, Michele had seventeen dances in the final show. She also had three dances to perform at the Perpich High School for Performing Arts as part of her graduation requirement. Her numerous costumes were disorganized and she was overwhelmed. One night in her room we sat on her bed, Michele in tears and me in decision mode. "We aren't going to do the mother/dancer dance this year," I told her. "Instead, I am going to become your personal assistant." We organized her costumes, planned the order of her dances, and often with giggles had more fun than if I had insisted on dancing with her for her senior gala.

In 2008, Michele's daughter Callidora, barely three years old, joined our family of dancers. By now I was beyond my first goal of clogging until I was 60. I knew that the pounding of clogging took a toll on knees. However, I loved dance too much to quit. I was still working the front desk at the studio. Listening to the music and seeing the delight of dancers of all ages made it imperative to stay. Also, Calli gave me an excuse for a new goal, to clog until I could do a four-generation dance. Four years later, the four of us entered stage left with five other mothers and daughters. When the music started, I thought, *I am really doing it. We four are all dancing!* Then I missed a step and decided I had better concentrate on my moves. Eventually, my next goal, dancing until I was 70, came and went. Our four-generation dance became a tradition, more joyfully fun with every passing year.

On August 13, 2012, I was rear-ended by a distracted driver who never braked before hitting me. I went from dancing five dances in the studio's May gala to not being able to walk to the end of my cul-de-sac without crying from pain. After a few days of feeling sorry for myself, I said out loud to no one but me, "Dammit, I am going to dance again!" I started with twice a week visits to my chiropractor and biweekly massages. Then I made an appointment at Rejuv Medical Center in Saint Cloud with a nonsurgical orthopedic specialist. When his assistant said they would start with my upper back and arms, I said, "No. I want you to do my legs first. I am a dancer." The doctor chuckled when he came in and agreed to start treatments on my lower back and legs. I hobbled into that first treatment and walked out with much less pain and increased mobility. The next week we added physical therapy after the treatments. For months I continued with the doctor, physical therapy, and chiropractic care on a weekly and then biweekly schedule.

When dance started in September, I sat on a stool and moved my feet to the steps as we learned them. I gradually progressed to dancing intermittently by the barre bar, my arms taking most of my weight off my legs. When the pain became intense, I returned to my stool. The night I danced a full class with no support, my teacher said she wasn't sure I could make it to the door of the studio, I looked so exhausted. I sat in my car in tears, more from joy that I could dance than from pain. I credit my recovery to my love of dance. I don't think I would have pushed myself that hard without my passion for dance to keep me going. My legs didn't go as high during the gala performance that year, but I danced my two class dances and our four-generation dance.

On June 15, 2013, ten months after my accident, I danced on the banks of the Mississippi River by the Stone Arch Bridge with groups of other dancers. We coordinated our 7:00 performance to those of other dancers in sixty cities around the world to bring attention to the need for clean water for all. Our group did a modern dance depicting the cycles of water: from drought and famine to rain bringing life-giving water to rivers, lakes, and watering holes. I felt connected to a global network of dancers making a difference while doing what we loved.

When I turned 75, I casually mentioned to one of the dance assistants, "You know, I should do a senior solo. After all, who is more senior than I am?" High school seniors did a solo dance as part of their farewell to the studio since many would be moving to different cities for college. She told other assistants, and before I could say, "What was I thinking?" I was committed. I have to confess here that I have never gotten over my fear of dancing on stage. I love it and am terrified at the same time. I have often said that I will perform until I get over my fear and do one dance perfectly, adding that at the rate I am going, I will probably be 100 and still saying the same thing!

Michele and Calli found the perfect dance *Hey Hey Hey* by Michael Franti. As I listened to the lyrics, I said, "This message is like the poem I created for my retirement, the need to live every day fully. It's perfect." Michele choreographed a clogging dance for me. I practiced like never before, wondering what possessed me to put myself through this torture. Then the fun took over! The dance assistants asked if they could dance with me at the end of the dance. The women in my class also wanted to be a part of my *solo*. My family had to be a part. Of course, I said *yes* to everyone.

On the night of my performance, I did the first half of the dance alone. I stood in a spotlight on stage with my back to the audience while Colleen, the dance school owner, introduced me. I panicked. Then I thought of my granddaughter's words of wisdom, "It's a solo; you can do whatever you want, and the audience will never know the difference." The music started, I turned around and let the dance direct my feet. When I danced to the side of the stage to bring Christine, Michele, and Calli on stage to join me, Michele, had her new baby boy Reed wrapped to the front of her body. The audience oohed and aahed with delight. A bit later, my class came on wearing multi-colored feather boas and presented each of us with one. Finally, the dance assistants, also with boas, joined us for the end of the dance. My solo turned into a fabulous production with thirty people joining me on stage! Fun surpasses fear any day. Asher, Michele's seven-year-old son, not wanting to dance, presented me with flowers at the end so he could be a part of the production. It was the best birthday celebration ever!

In 2018 Asher began dancing in a boys' hip-hop class. Calli is into hip-hop, and also in a performing group. Michele teaches some of their classes. Reed listens to the music and dances in the lobby. My new goal is to enjoy every single year that I can still dance. I joke that when I am 100, I will do another solo, probably with the boas decorating my walker. My family, the women in my class, and the dance assistants all promise they will be back to dance again with me. In the meantime, I am still dancing and plan to continue our four-generation clogging dance. I am working at the front desk, still delighting in the dance assistants and dancers. And, my now famous mint brownies are baked to celebrate another dance year with the staff. Each time I dance, I think of Mom, of the way her body felt and moved to her internal music. I picture us on the day she, too, got to experience the joy of dance.

Chapter 16

Continued Care Meetings

November 2011

Alzheimer's continued its relentless invasion of Mom's brain. I pictured it like some horror movie, a monster eating her brain in the dark of night to the backdrop of a raging thunderstorm. Unlike in the movies, I knew this heroine wouldn't survive.

One day Mom started choking on her apple fritter that we had brought as a treat. Patty patted her on the back, and I gave her something to drink. She continued to have minor problems with her eating. Normally, I would have been more concerned, wondering if this was one more progression toward her not knowing how to eat, to her muscles not getting the command to swallow. I would picture one more hole in her assaulted brain, one more short circuit. But today, I smiled, happy that she could choke. The seemingly strange perspective arose from another meeting the previous week with Dr. Faber.

I had arrived early to the conference room and watched a woman set up a phone system so Sharon could be with us through a speaker phone. I chuckled as my mind drifted back to when I had placed a phone on an upturned wastebasket. Soon Mary came, coffee in hand, then Patty, then the nurse, the social worker, the activities director, all of the people who kept Mom healthy, active, and comfortable. Dr. Faber entered, shook our hands, and explained that Minnesota required a meeting to meet new state requirements for nursing homes.

While I listened to him talk, I thought it could almost be a recording, his favorite analogy of trying to reroute around construction zones. I have to admit, having driven through detours that were in themselves under construction and further detoured me, I could picture what was happening to Mom's brain circuitry. The meeting reiterated much of what we already had gone through: no resuscitation, no intubation, comfort care at the end.

Then we came to a new point. Dr. Faber recommended no antibiotic care if Mom got pneumonia, a disease that frequently was the cause of death for Alzheimer's patients. The discussion became animated, Sharon's voice equally heard along with ours. We wanted her treated for any infectious disease. She had already recovered from one pneumonia bout. Dr. Faber explained that if Mom couldn't cough up the fluid in her lungs, if the Alzheimer's had progressed to that point, no amount of antibiotics would help. We would be prolonging her agony. But, we insisted, she now could cough. Once again, we were confronted with the reality of a disease that progressed weekly if not daily. We could easily chart her decline over the past few months. Still, we weren't ready to give a death sentence to a woman who could still walk, could talk (although much was unintelligible), could interact with us (I often was amazed at how she demanded an audience with eye contact, looking directly into our eyes until we responded). We weren't ready to give in on this point with her current health. As much as we had lost of our mother, we still loved her and wanted her to be part of our lives for as long as possible.

We ended the impasse with a compromise: the staff would always inform us of any health change, which they had consistently done already. Dr. Faber would order one round of antibiotics. If that didn't work, he would switch to palliative care. We always had the final say, he reminded us. We could change the order based on how Mom was doing. We agreed, he added that to the new state form, and we signed. The rest of the meeting was a more relaxed review of how Mom was doing.

With that meeting in mind, I watched Mom cough and choke on her food, both a sign of regression and a sign of hope that this disease hadn't taken that function away from her. I smiled, we helped her through her coughing bout, and gave her another bite of apple fritter. No choking this time. I could continue to do Mom's nails, we could soothe her face and arms with lotion, we could sing songs, laugh and empathize when she became sad. We could watch her interact with her doll when we left, Mom already unaware of our having been there. But she was still here, still alive, still Geri, my mom.

June 2012

When Patty and I walked into the Alzheimer's unit, I saw Mom across the room, head drooping with sleep, her doll baby in her arm, a bright orange-red robe that she wore for a sweater. I wondered where her blue sweater was, and perhaps if she chose a bright color to wear today. I approached her cautiously, wary of her reaction when we awakened her. The previous week I had experienced a hate I had never seen in her before.

Mary and I were sitting by the conference room, waiting for our monthly staff meeting when we noticed a worker walking Mom down the hallway from her room toward the commons area. When they got closer, the aide pointed to us and steered Mom toward us. Mary stood up and offered Mom her chair.

Mom glared at her and said, "You sit in it."

"I just wanted to give you a soft chair to sit in," Mary said.

"I'll throw a rock at you, too," Mom answered, "if you don't sit down." Hearing totally different words than Mary spoke, she responded with hate bordering on rage. Her face contorted, her eyes narrowed to slits as she glared at us. Then she walked away toward a man in a wheelchair. Touching his shoulder, she spoke to him with a tenderness that contrasted sharply with her interaction with us.

"That was interesting," said Mary.

The interaction became relevant for the conference because we were there to discuss changes in Mom's behavior in general and an incident report where Mom punched a volunteer who was redirecting a man who had wandered into Mom's room. The person wasn't hurt, and it reminded us of the times that Mom would punch us in the arm when she was angry with us.

I thought of the time I laughed at another lady whom we called the *stealth thief*. She could grab onto things faster than we could react. That day, I was helping Mom eat her lunch. Patty whispered my name several times to get my attention and pointed to our *stealth thief*. She had taken a slice of bread from Mom's tray and was eating it with obvious relish, a smile of smug satisfaction on her face. I started to laugh. Thinking that I was laughing at her, Mom punched me on my arm, definitely not hard enough to hurt, but enough to let me know I was making her angry. I touched my forehead to hers and said, "Did I make you mad?" "Yes", she pouted. "I'm sorry," I said dropping my head slightly and looking into her eyes through the top of mine. We both smiled, and soon we were both laughing.

I likened it to a small child with limited vocabulary for emotions. The punch was her primary language to express her negative emotions. Since she didn't hit hard enough to do any harm, we thought little of the incident report, wondering instead if volunteers were well enough trained to work with Alzheimer's patients. This latest interaction caused us to rethink our reactions to the report.

During the meeting, the staff reassured us that their Geri was mostly pleasant and a joy to work with. Her obstinate episodes were fewer than those of most residents and part of the progression of the disease. Mom's health was excellent: she was still ambulatory, she could mostly feed herself, and she interacted well with the other residents. I thought of some conversations I had witnessed between Mom and other residents. Visual observation showed two people engaged in a pleasant conversation. Hearing them interact, each was talking about something totally different, yet conversing with each other as though they understood one another. I had stood there, mesmerized, wondering what was going through their minds. The conclusion of the meeting was that Mom was stable, even though her disease was noticeably progressing.

Now, I was apprehensive as I gently touched her arm to awaken her, our last encounter entrenched in my mind. "Hello, lovely lady," I smiled while Mom slowly focused and stared at us, trying to figure out what we were doing there. More and more I called her *my lovely lady*, the only name that could come close to a substitute for *Mom*. In her mind, she normally varied between teen and childhood years. During one visit, she started giggling and looked at Patty. "We almost got into trouble that time didn't we?" she told her. Patty giggled back. Then Mom went on about some school caper, her language not clear enough for us to understand, but her emotions and tone definitely giving us a glimpse into her teen years. Patty reacted like she knew what the caper was all about and the two of them had a delightful interaction while I watched. The person I knew as *Mom* definitely did not fit this person I was seeing.

We gave her the strawberry banana smoothie we had brought. Then we broke off pieces of cake as a further treat. Just as Mom used to use food to make us feel good when we were young, we now used food to make her smile and interact more with us. When she drifted away from us, our touching her glass in a *Cheers!* toast brought her back. Her smile or laughter at our toast added joy to our visit.

Back home, I went through another of my frequent quests to understand this horrid disease and who my mother had become because of it. Her reaction to Mary looked visceral, not rationally emotional. It was an instant, instinctive reaction to a supposed threat. I always maintained that our visits, while instantly forgotten, left an emotional positive affect that could brighten Mom's day. Now I questioned if our *Cheers!* and laughter brought out anything more than a pat on the head or a kind word would elicit a response from an animal. Was it nothing more than a Pavlovian interaction we now had with the techniques we used to get Mom to interact with us? When I polished her nails, was she simply responding to touch? Our last effort to get Mom to choose a nail color was pathetically humorous. She couldn't choose a bottle, so we put three different colors on Patty's nails. Instead of picking one, she traced Patty's fingers and started on one of her stories. Then she rubbed my arm, creating another story. We eventually picked the color. While I was polishing her nails, she started laughing and said, "Look," pointing to her doll. I looked and faked a laugh. She was again seeing something happening that we didn't. Her world distanced more from us each time we saw her. Her brain continually lost more and more functioning. I loved my mother; I wanted to protect her from this progression; but I felt so helpless, so ineffectual. I intensely hated what Alzheimer's could and had done. It felt as visceral as Mom's reaction to Mary.

Chapter 17

My Spiritual Journey

Even as a child, I determined that once I left the harsh punishment and derisive abuse of my father, I would never follow rules unless they made sense to me. That willfulness carried over into my spiritual life, leading me from strict Catholicism to becoming a spiritual explorer.

I sat at the kitchen table in a farmhouse country home, listening to the shaman explain his traditions and how he performed Inipi sweat lodge ceremonies. Sandy colored hair on this thin, agile man separated him from the Native American heritage I had expected. However, I soon learned he had been trained by Black Elk and lived by Native values. My friend Barbara had suggested this evening as a spiritual new beginning to my life as a single, divorced woman after thirty-five years of marriage. So here I was, starting a new century, 2000, and celebrating my fifty-eighth birthday learning new traditions and meeting new people.

Clumsily, I tried to tie the twenty-one, one-inch red cotton squares around tobacco without breaking the thread that tied all together and without my knot coming undone and dumping my tobacco back onto the table. Silently, I saged each small bit of tobacco, letting the smoke from the sage stick set my intent into each one, the first fourteen for blessings I wanted for the world around me and for other people. Only the last seven could be personal. Here and in the lodge, I was told, we put others' intentions before our own. The smell of fish soup cooking on the stove mixed with the sweet smell of redwood tobacco.

Once we were in the lodge and the canvas was pulled over the door, the only light came from the stones in the center pit, the ancient ones, glowing hot from the fire outside the lodge, ready for water to be poured over them to begin the ritual. In this lodge three rounds of rocks were brought in, each round increasing the intensity of the steamy heat. The shaman began with a message for the prayer of that round; then he passed his ceremonial pipe, allowing each of us to smoke it and add our prayers to his. In the mystery round he would bring us messages from the Great Spirit, either for our own lives or ways in which we were to help others. The ceremony was intense, both physically and spiritually. When I exited the lodge, I felt a soul-deep peace that had eluded me for a long time. While we shared food to ground us for our individual journeys home, I marveled at the love and friendship I felt from these people who had been strangers only hours before. I knew I would incorporate these ceremonies into my new life.

During my years as a strict Catholic, I could never have fathomed myself in such a ceremony. That would make me a heathen, creating a sure path to hell. Growing up with the rules and regulations of Catholicism, I incorporated them into my being. The black-and-white doxology was simple to follow. The results were guaranteed; living a good life meant heaven. Bad behaviors led to hell, or at least purgatory, that in-between place where after death I would continue to atone for my sins.

I attended Catholic grade school, Ascension in North Minneapolis for my first six grades and Our Lady of the Lake in Mound after we moved. My earliest memories involved strict rules. To receive communion, one had to fast from midnight on. At my first communion, the nuns had covered the water fountains at school where we gathered before our ceremonious walk to church. A sip of water could ban us from receiving Christ that day. We had to fold our hands in prayer, pointing to heaven. If we let them slip down, we were praying to the devil and would go to hell. Fridays meant no meat, hence the classic tuna noodle casserole or grilled cheese and tomato soup suppers. During Lent, we said the rosary after supper every night. This structure created a framework in which I grew to have a personal relationship with God. I would simply talk to Him as much as I would pray my formal prayers. Since Ascension was a mere three blocks from home, I walked to church early most mornings to attend Mass before school.

At Our Lady of the Lake, I joined the choir. The songs resonated soul deep. When in eighth grade I was chosen to crown Mary with a wreath of flowers on May first, I was ecstatic. I walked at the head of a procession from the school, down the block and across the street to where a statue of Mary sat in the churchyard. I stood on tiptoe and placed the wreath on her head, feeling especially blessed. For confirmation, I dutifully memorized the catechism so I wouldn't embarrass my church and family when the bishop asked me questions in front of everyone at the service to be sure I was ready. The rules guided my religious life after confirmation. On All Souls Day, November 2, we could get souls out of purgatory by praying a prescribed litany for them. However, we could only get one soul out per visit. I, and many others, would walk into church, get one soul out, walk out of church and down the block far enough to be off of church property, do a U-turn and walk back in for the next soul. I'd repeat that until I had exhausted my list of dead people that I knew.

Though I didn't realize it then, my religion was highly judgmental and what I would now call quite arrogant. My Lutheran friends would never see God like we Catholics; they could be happy in limbo, but would never see the face of God. Who knew what would happen to the Holy Rollers down the block, whose loud shouts and songs drifted into our Masses. Even as a child, I couldn't understand how pagan children and their families could be condemned to hell when they hadn't even heard about Jesus. Then I heard about *baptism of desire*, which gave a lot of latitude. If people really wanted to be good, but had not yet had the opportunity to be saved, they could go to limbo with the Lutherans. I was relieved that God would not make all of these poor people suffer. Throughout my high school years, my beliefs would deepen into a spirituality that included helping others, living a good life, and talking to God as if He were a personal friend, not simply my ruler and judge.

Ironically, it was my Catholic college education at the College of Saint Benedict that led to my seriously questioning my religion. My religion course included an exploration of world religions where I saw many similarities along with the differences. "How can you choose to be a Catholic if you don't know what else there is so you can know what you are choosing?" our instructor asked us.

For me, who had been fearfully obedient, this was revolutionary! I now felt knowledgeable in choosing Catholicism. It fulfilled my soul deep needs. With the church located between my dorm and my classes, I would pop into church daily and say, "Hi God. It's me Barb. Have a nice day."

I learned one day how much the liberal nuns aggravated the conservative bishop of Saint Cloud. For a senior paper in philosophy, I had chosen to study Sartre. Because he was on a banned list, I had to write the bishop for permission. I made the horrible mistake of formatting my letter in modern form without indentation and addressing the bishop as *sir* rather than your *excellency*. I also had a spelling mistake, the final straw. I was called to the dean's office from lunch, a sure sign I was in trouble. The bishop had written her a scathing letter admonishing her to train her students in proper etiquette rather than allowing them to read trash. She showed no anger toward me or the bishop. Rather she suggested that we compose a letter of apology together. While it grated on me to apologize to this arrogant person, I was more than happy to help the dean redeem herself with someone who imposed his rules on her too. Her secretary typed the letter to be sure it was perfectly correct. I wrote my paper on Albert Camus, who was less well known than Sartre and therefore had flown under the church radar. My respect for the nuns and their deep spirituality, combined with their worldly wisdom, guided my life from then on.

My Catholic religion gave me a spiritual community during my early married life and while raising my children. It taught my children that more existed than the life we knew. It gave them guiding principals for their actions. It comforted them when their brother Douglas died. In the 1970s I became involved in the education department, eventually becoming president of the board of education of Saint Andrews's Church in Brainerd, Minnesota. Joe became a communion minister. We became an integral part of a community with similar values and beliefs. Still, doubts began to creep into my acceptance of church dogma.

I first balked at the church's stance on contraception. Back in Casselton I had watched a casual friend become more psychotic with each of her five deliveries. Her husband pleaded for dispensation to use contraception. It was denied. She ended up permanently in a mental institution after chasing her young children around the kitchen with a knife while cutting herself. Her husband was left to raise five traumatized children alone. It didn't seem right or just to me. In Brainerd, a good friend had five children under the age of seven. She was physically and emotionally exhausted. Several days a week I visited her to support her and give her someone to talk to beyond toddlers. While the children slept, we drank tea in comfy chairs and chatted. When my son died, I knew that after birthing three children in three years, I was physically and emotionally unready to chance another pregnancy. I didn't even ask for permission. Contraception was my first act of defiance.

Another problem for me was the church's attitude toward homosexuality. When a friend's high school daughter confided in me that she was lesbian, my only thought was to convince her that I saw a wonderful person in her. I knew from her mother that she had already attempted suicide. "You have no idea what it is like to walk into church and be told you are damned for who you are," she told me. I could only tell her how wrong the church was in that message, that she was in no way damned.

I wanted to cry for her, and for the woman who taught me racquetball at the Y, and for the thousands like them who in the 1970s had no place to go for acceptance. I could picture Jesus crying with us. This was not what He had taught. This was in no way Christian. How many beautiful, productive lives were thwarted because of religious bias. I began to wonder how I could still support my church while silently trying to help those whom it condemned.

When we moved to Coon Rapids in 1978, I again became active in religious education, this time facilitating confirmation classes, including those of my children. Joe worked many Sundays and became less active in the church. When the abortion protest movement took hold, I again questioned how Christian this really was. Where the church saw abortion as a moral issue, I saw it as also being a social issue. A wealthy woman could go anywhere to anonymously get an abortion, and return to her community and church with no one being aware of her actions. Women in poverty were the ones using coat hangers and going to back door doctors who often left them with infections or worse. What would happen, I wondered, if we spent as much effort and money to assure that those children who were already born had a roof over their heads and food on their tables? What would happen if we showed those women compassion rather than condemnation? While I could not consider abortion for myself, I could not judge someone in whose shoes I had not walked. At this point, I began to look beyond Catholicism for my spiritual fulfillment.

Starting in the late 1990s, I annually attended a week-long IIIHS (International Institute of Integral Human Sciences) spiritual conference during my summers. Among other offerings, I chose workshops in Reiki healing, qigong, meditation, and spiritual art. Sharon came with me the second year to see what my spirituality was like, being concerned about my no longer attending Mass. She saw it to be compatible with her Catholicism, especially when several nuns joined us in some or our workshops.

In 1999, a well-known Canadian psychic gave a large group presentation on the stage of the auditorium. After her presentation, she walked the aisles giving messages to individual people in the audience. She stopped by me and said, "You are going to be a teacher." When I told her that I was a high school teacher, she said, "That is not what I mean. You are going to be a spiritual teacher." Then she looked at Sharon and said, "You will be a healer." Sharon had no intention of doing any healing work. However, she later became a Reiki healing master, taking advanced instruction after her initial taste at a later conference and follow-up with a spiritual group that formed in her community.

At the same conference, I decided to have a spiritual reading by a Native holy woman. During our session, she said she saw a raven mask covering my head and face so that I looked through the eyes of the raven. She further said that it had already been with me and would continue to be a special guide and protector for me. I took the raven as a spirit animal, an energy guide who came to me often throughout my life, especially when I was in distress.

When the IIIHS conferences ended because of financial problems, Sharon and I went on a summer solstice retreat in New Mexico in 2003. We entered the week's activities through a kiva, a Southwestern version of a sweat lodge, made out of clay. Like in the sweat lodge ceremonies, participants prayed to the four directions, the difference being that in each direction a statue of the blessed virgin Mary sat next to the symbol of that direction. It confirmed my belief that what I was doing was a fulfillment of my church upbringing, not a contradiction. I left my childlike blind obedience to rules behind and entered spiritual adulthood.

During that week we had spiritual guidance seminars and maintained silent meditation after supper. We rafted down the Rio Chama River, navigating rapids between a three and four difficulty level and jumping into the water at the moment of solstice. Halfway up Changing Woman Mountain, we drummed with crystals that we got from what seemed like a carpet of clear quartz. On the last night we walked into the White Canyon and watched the sun set and the stars come out, at first only a few, then sparkling like crystals in the sky when it became dark. Then we were told that we were to find our way out of the canyon alone. I wasn't ready for that surprise. When it was my turn, I stumbled along the path, trying to feel my way in the pitch-black darkness. I couldn't even see the white walls that surrounded me. The stars that had looked so bright and twinkly a short time ago now looked dim and distant. Gradually, I began to feel the rhythm of the earth beneath me. I let my body rise and fall with the ruts and rises; I shifted from side to side with the unevenness of the path's borders. My body moved with the same fluidity as it had in the raft, becoming one with the earth as it had become one with the waves and current. Sharon had more difficulty than I did. When her fear seemed to overcome her, one of the leaders would appear at her side encouraging her, then disappear, leaving her to navigate the trail alone again. For both of us, ancient grandmothers appeared to us while we walked. We both clearly saw them smiling encouragement and direction when we were unsure of our path. This journey tested our courage, our faith, our spiritual awakening, and our trust in Mother Earth. At the end, after successfully walking out of the canyon alone, Sharon and I agreed that it was an amazing experience, a grand finale to our week.

Beginning in 2007, Sharon and I attended annual workshops in chakra clearing, often with the same people who accompanied us to New Mexico. We learned to maintain our own energy and relate to others while grounded in that energy. Working on my throat chakra gave me courage to write honestly. In difficult situations, I would picture an energy pole running through my chakras, connecting me to heaven and earth. It helped me to honor people who disagreed with me without compromising myself.

When Americo, a South American shaman, came to Minneapolis, my friend Barbara arranged for me to do a healing ceremony with him. After the healing, I had a lucid dream. I was walking in the hilly forests of California. Deep into the woods, I fell and broke my leg. While I lay there, a cougar came and dragged me by the neck to a stream so I could drink water. It lay by me at night to keep me warm. At dawn, it was gone. In the cougar's place was a shaman with a cane that curved into a carved cougar head at the top. He did a healing ceremony on my leg and left. Still I couldn't walk. I continued to drink from the stream. That night, the cougar came again. For three nights and days, the same routine followed. On the third day, the shaman told me I was healed, I could walk out of the woods. When I told him I wanted to stay, that I felt so safe and spiritually alive, he told me I needed to leave, that I had much work left to do in the world. I walked out of the woods and into a town.

When I told my friend Barbara about the dream, she told me that Americo was known as the man who sleeps with jaguars, the South American cousin of my cougar! I decided to attend his week-long retreat on the West Coast. The scheduled location on Vancouver Island had to be moved because Canada wasn't allowing South American Indians into the country, perhaps because Americo didn't have a visa. I never knew why. I flew into Seattle, rented a car, and drove down the California coast to a Buddhist monastery, the new destination of the retreat. When I drove into the complex, I stared, breathless. The landscape was identical to the woods I had seen in my dream! I had many spiritual awakenings that week. The cougar became my second spirit animal.

At the same time, I took a year long shamanic feng shui class and began doing many house clearings. In each, I told people that what they wished for would happen; however, it might not come in the way they expect. When we cleaned out my parents' attic, I refused to add a feng shui component to the cleaning. Only if someone asked and knew what to expect would I do that. Instead, I prayed that our cleaning might lighten the heaviness they were both experiencing.

In the early 2000s, I also began adding a spiritual component to my jewelry making, designing zodiac bracelets and anklets with stones whose energies resonated with the sun, moon, and ascendant signs of a person's birthdate. When a friend was diagnosed with terminal cancer and given six months to two years to live, I created a healing bracelet for her. She wore it throughout her treatment. She amazed the doctors by conquering the cancer. On the day she was declared cancer free, the bracelet broke. She asked me to fix it. Instead, I told her the stones had done their work; I buried them and made her a new one.

These are but a few of many experiences along my spiritual journeys. Throughout, I felt more like an explorer, wanting to incorporate everything into my being. Often, I was my own biggest skeptic, yet over and over again, healing, growth, and miracles occurred that couldn't be put off as coincidence. It happened too consistently, too many times.

Scientifically, we all are combinations of energy. I believe that the energies of the earth, the rocks and stones, the trees, the birds, the animals, the sky, and other humans all flow through me. When I honor that unity, when I work with that energy, miracles happen. I don't believe in panaceas. Rather, I believe that God, the Great Spirit, created this wonderful, universal energy synergy. When I live consciously, listening to the voice of spirit within, I am more spiritually fulfilled, more at peace with the world around me. My daily life becomes joyful, even in difficult times. I will continue to journey wherever that spirit leads me. I still continue to say "Good morning God; it's me Barb. Have a nice day." Now I also add a prayer of thanks for each wondrous day.

While my mother would never accept my spirituality while she was cognizant, it became a way for us to communicate when she advanced into Alzheimer's. I could connect energetically with her when words failed. My lifelong spiritual path that continuously led me further from my mother, in the end, brought me full circle to a closeness with her that I otherwise wouldn't have had.

Chapter 18

Mom's Birthdays

Birthdays were our way to celebrate Mom's life and bring her extra joy and festivities along with gifts, cake and ice cream. It was Alzheimer's way to dampen our celebrations with yearly signs of its relentless progress.

Mom's 85th to 89th Birthdays
2007-2011

Birthdays graphically marked the progression of Mom's Alzheimer's. When she turned 85, she was living at Waterford. Patty suggested a big party, probably the last time Mom could interact with everyone. Already signs of her diminished memory functioning were evident. We decided to rent a hall, brought in our own food, made floral centerpieces for the tables and invited people from our early years on Dupont Avenue along with Mom's present-day family and friends. Several of the children who had lived next door to our first house, now adults, came to visit. Neighbors from Mom's last home in Robbinsdale came to tell her how much they missed her. Among her many presents, Christine gave her a large birthday bag filled with yarn. Mom *oohed and aahed* at the many colors while she fondled the soft skeins. She would never use the yarn, her memory no longer telling her how to create the stitches that she had crocheted a myriad of times. Instead, she would keep the yarn by her living room chair, enjoying their colors and touch.

By the time Mom celebrated her 86th, 87th, 88th, and 89th birthdays, she was in a locked ward at North Ridge nursing home. Always a family for celebrations, we organized parties in a commons room on her floor, complete with cake, balloons, and flowers. What do you buy a woman who still likes lipstick, perfume and pretty clothes, but has the mind of a toddler? Where in this dichotomy do you fit a birthday present? Among the presents I remember were new blouses and a necklace Mom could put on over her head since she could no longer use a clasp. I got her new nail polish for our manicures and several junior puzzles with large-sized pieces. Let us not forget the wind up chicken that delighted her long after she knew how to wind it herself! Sharon gave Mom an old doll, covered in ground-in dirt from years of play, a few wisps of hair clinging to a bald head. *What a strange gift*, I thought. Yet this gift proved to be the best of all. It became Mother's child, her confidant, her comfort when she was agitated. The aides would clean it and share stories with Mom while she cradled it. One day an aide took me aside and said, "My baby grew out of her sleepers so I brought your mother a couple so she could change her doll's clothes." The pride in her voice matched the loving look she gave the doll. What was this doll's power? I never could figure out its magic. I only know it was coveted by other Alzheimer's patients, loved by all who saw it, and became as human a person for Mom to relate to as we were, sometimes even more so than us.

Mom was moved into an Alzheimer's ward in March of 2010 and celebrated her 89th birthday in April of 2011. We had a celebration in the party room which adjoined a court-yard where the kids could play outdoors if the end-of-April weather cooperated. A door closed off the noise of our partying. I made Mom a purple and green fluorite necklace, long enough to put over her head, because of its healing energy, which could calm Mom's agitation and make her Alzheimer's progression gentler. Where previous necklaces had been inexpensive, the natural stones made this one very expensive. I was aware that not only did Mom hide things, but also things traveled from one resident's room to another. We frequently found Mom's stuffed animals in other rooms or the commons area. I decided that the necklace would bring its energy where it was needed. It would travel around the complex but spend most of its time in Mom's room. Mom enjoyed the festivities and interacted individually with us. Then we lit the birthday candles and started singing *Happy Birthday*. Mom burst out sobbing. "Why didn't my mother come?" she asked. Throughout her life she'd had a complex relationship with her mother. Grandma Lindsay was often more my mother than Mom. Her tough German demeanor seemed to diminish Mom, yet Mom depended on her to help out. When I was ten, Grandma started to live with us part of the time and with her son in Texas the rest of the time. Mom was relieved to have her own home back but then felt lost, almost abandoned when Grandma left. Perhaps this is what triggered her current emotions. We soothed Mom as best we could, blew out her candles, and brought her back to the present and a good mood with birthday cake. We were used to these sudden shifts in moods and time. However, it bothered us more at this festive time.

Mom's 90th Birthday
DNA Connections
2012

One day, when Mom's Alzheimer's was troubling me, I talked to a spiritual advisor who had mentored me for decades.

"Your mother is fulfilling what she came on this earth to accomplish but couldn't do in the life she led. Beyond the Alzheimer's, she is operating on another plane. She is finishing her life's work. You know, you could communicate with her on that other plane." We talked about the chakra energy centers of the body. He then showed me how to block my third chakra, the one that lets in the rest of the world, and then meditate in order to join my DNA to Mom's, opening up communication lines.

I sat quietly taking this all in. I have a strong belief that we decide on the other side what we come into this world to achieve. We know what we have left undone in our many life cycles. Those we know on the other side, what many call *heaven,* offer to be by us and help us. Whether we call them *spirit guides, angels,* or *saints,* they are with us on this earth journey. Once we are born, we consciously forget this purpose.

I also had experienced other planes when meditating. I celebrated my solar return birthdays, calculating when the first breath of my birth would occur each year. It was a spiritual New Year's, letting go of any past difficulties or hurts, and calling in what I hoped to accomplish in the coming year. One year, it occurred at 2:43 AM. Not wanting to stay up or wake the rest of the household with an alarm clock, I feared I would miss this one. Nevertheless, before falling asleep, I prayed that I would wake up in time. At 2:30 AM I felt a gentle touch to my right shoulder. *It's time to wake up,* a voice whispered. During that meditation, I was transported to another plane where I heard shouts of joy and congratulations for this birthday and for my courage to come into this earth journey. I saw these beings as points of light, moving and communicating much like we would at a festive party. When I returned to my earth body, a sense of immense joy and peace stayed with me.

On another occasion, when I visited my ninety-year-old mother-in-law, a strict, conservative Catholic, she looked at me and said, "I can't tell this to anyone else. They would think I was crazy or demented. Three nights ago, when I went to bed, you were there. You tucked me in and kissed me good night."

I assured her that she did see me. "I astral travel when I sleep," I told her. "Most often I have no memory of where I have been, only a sense of having helped someone. I am sure I really did tuck you in, even if not physically so."

After our session, I thanked my mentor, slightly doubtful about consciously trying what had been an unconscious experience. However, I used the process to remotely tuck Mom in each night. Then, two incidents occurred that convinced me that my spiritual communication was working.

When I was visiting a friend in Arizona, we went to a musical review that took me back to childhood memories of music I had heard over the radio. It also reminded me of Mom's joy when we took her to plays and Broadway musicals. For whatever reason, I quietly put my right hand over my third chakra, the way I did at night to connect to Mom, and began describing all the music and artists, who were projected on a screen on stage. "I know you would love this if you could be here," I told her. The entire production was spent reminiscing and somehow sharing those memories with Mom. Perhaps, I thought, it was simply my romanticizing the moment.

On my first visit to Mom after returning, she looked at me and said, "I know you; you're Barbara". I smiled at her and said, "Yes. And you are my lovely lady". She hadn't known me for years and immediately forgot who I was. *Could it be my other plane communication*, I thought. I believed it was and also believed it wasn't possible.

Later, when Mom celebrated her 90th birthday, we again planned a large family party in the family room. My niece's confirmation ended up being scheduled that same day, so we arranged times to accommodate both.

I once again thought of Mom, who was missing this spiritual event for a favorite grandchild. Once again I covered my third chakra and described the entire service to Mom as it happened. I described the stole her granddaughter had made and how she looked as she was confirmed. I described the sunlight shining through the windows. When I was done, I said "See you soon, Mom. It's your birthday."

The day was warm and beautiful, the children enjoying playing outside, the rest of us partying around Mom more than with her. When Christine phoned me, asking how to get into the locked ward, I said I'd come get her. We chatted and slowly walked the hallway to the Alzheimer's area. When we got to the party, everyone was excitedly looking at Mom and then at me. "You missed it," they said, talking all at once. "After you left, Mom looked around and said, *Where is Barbara?* She looked around again and said, *I know Barbara was here. I saw her.*

I did miss the moment. She no longer knew me, slipping back into her own world. We partied, fed her cake and juice, and after a while let an aide take her back to her room. She was exhausted from all the commotion. We stayed a while longer, each family gradually leaving. We sisters cleaned the room, being the last to leave.

I only used the extended DNA communication with Mom for these two events because they seemed important to her. I continued to tuck her in spiritually at night, sometimes talking a bit and then mentally kissing her goodnight. She never knew me other than those two times. Coincidence? I don't think so.

After those incidents, whenever I saw her revisit past experiences in her life, I was more convinced than ever that she was healing from past events in her life while she soaked up the love and care of the nurses and aides who showered her with hugs, love, and the attention she craved but didn't get during her cognizant life. I still hate this strange disease. I still wish it hadn't taken my mother from me. But I also believe in a higher plane than my awareness can comprehend. Whatever Mom's journey, I am on the outside, seldom able to share her world. Perhaps that is part of my journey.

Mom's 91st Birthday
2013

What a difference a year makes, or two weeks, or even a day. On Sunday, April 28, we all gathered in the party room as we had the year before, Mary bringing a cake and fun presents. When I got there, Mom was sleeping, her head back, her mouth open. She reminded me of the way Dad looked when I saw him after he died, lying on the garage floor. Perhaps it's how we all look with our heads back, deep in sleep. In spite of the noise from the kids, Mom couldn't stay awake. We partied, and she slept. Patty got her awake enough to eat a small piece of cake. It seemed strange to watch all of us partying, talking, eating, drinking, the kids running in and out to the courtyard to play while Mom slept in the center of it all. *This was truly more for us than for her*, I kept thinking. *Just like Dr. Faber had told us about our visits.* Before today, I knew he was wrong. Affectively, Mom enjoyed the attention. While we could be anyone, she enjoyed our coming to see her. Today, we gathered one more time for one more birthday, a family tradition that revolved around Mom. Much like the center of a wheel, she remained still, unmoved, while we spun around her.

Mary brought a soft rubbery ball with rubber fringes, much like the one that had shrunk to a hard mass during its decontamination because of a flu outbreak. I couldn't find a replacement at first, and then decided that Mom no longer played ball. Mary, bless her Pollyanna heart, found one with a smiley face on it. I started throwing it and soon several of us were playing catch. I stood in front of Mom and threw it to her. Others did too. She caught it two or three times before nodding off. Another present was a soft green throw that Mom had knitted almost thirty years ago for Mary's daughter, Crystal. It had been handed down in her family and now made its way back to Mom, who caressed it with her fingers while she slept. Worn and stained, it was by far the best present of the day. It reminded me of the doll Sharon had given Mom and which Mom still cherished.

The day before our big party, Mary and I had come to see Mom on April 27, her actual birthday.

"I'm going to visit Mom on Saturday and bring her an ice cream treat. I know she doesn't know the difference, but she shouldn't spend her birthday alone," Mary told me. I thought about it after our phone conversation ended and decided that I wanted to go with her.

My dance recital was the following weekend, so I wouldn't see Mom then. I called Mary back. "I'd like to go with you," I said. "I'll do her nails and hair to get her ready for Sunday." Mom was tired but laughed with us and told stories we pretended to understand. She couldn't sing the words to our songs. I'd noticed that more and more she'd hum a few lines, the words eluding her. She still smiled and swayed to the music.

While I watched Mom sleep during Sunday's party, I was glad I had gone the previous day, when she was more alert. I was even happier that we had decided to celebrate her birthday a few weeks earlier when Sharon and Bob could come to visit. Mom had laughed and interacted with us, sang bits of songs with us, and thoroughly enjoyed the attention she was getting. Bob took pictures of us four sisters and Mom on Mary's cell phone, and Mary took one of Bob and Sharon with Mom. It was a grand party! Now, I could really appreciate what a special gift that was.

On the day of her birthday celebration, we also noticed that occasionally Mom would hold her left breast and either moan slightly or gasp a bit, having been diagnosed with nipple cancer. It was obviously starting to bother her. The nurse brought her two Tylenol. I thought about the arthritis in my wrists and how little Tylenol would affect the pain. She would soon need stronger pain medications. We would have to watch to see that she was taken care of. While we couldn't and wouldn't do any treatment for the cancer, we were adamant that she be spared pain as much as possible. Once again I prayed that however she died, it would be gentle. Only this time I knew I prayed for her, and not to spare my watching her deteriorate. Recently, I had found myself crying unexpectedly, knowing how much I would miss her. At the same time, I knew again, it needed to be about her, about accepting what I had no control over, and about bringing as much joy and as little pain as possible to her remaining days.

Before we left, I gave Mom one last hug, noticing that lately I cradled her in my arms more than I hugged her. She cuddled my arm and rested her head on my shoulder, much like an infant would when tired. I stood there and held her until an aide came to take her to her room. Then I joined the others outside in the warmest sunshine we'd had that spring.

Chapter 19

A Fall Leads to Final Goodbyes

August, 2013

It was inevitable. Yet at some level I expected Mom to keep living, to keep smiling when she saw us, to keep holding her doll and talking to it. A fall too suddenly shattered that delusion, that hope. Yet in the midst of grieving came angels and butterflies to comfort us while we said goodbye.

I had just put my suitcase in the trunk of my car, ready to head north to Brainerd to visit friends, when Patty called.

"Mom fell and broke her hip," she said. "She tried to get out of bed some time between three and five this morning."

Immediately I thought of how many times a fall meant the end, especially in older people, and Mom was 91.

"They've got her on OxyContin so she's not in pain."

For years I had asked for a directive to be put in Mom's medical file so she could get stronger pain medication than Tylenol. For years the answer was the same: it was only a quick phone call to get any medication needed. "What about weekends?" I had asked. All agreed everything was more difficult with the regular staff gone. Still, nothing had been done.

Then, on a Saturday a couple of weeks before, Mary and I visited Mom to bring her new slippers, her old ones once again shrunken from laundering. We noticed her wincing and shifting her weight in her wheelchair. When we went to put on her new slippers, her legs were so huge from excess water, we immediately called a nurse to see what was happening and gave permission to cut her pants if they got any tighter. We took Mom back to her room, hoping that her regular chair might be more comfortable for her. Since Patty had medical power of attorney, and since she was playing up North, we made Mom as comfortable as we could and left to call Patty to see if she was aware of the situation. While every minor bruise or incident had previously warranted a call, no one had contacted her this time. We told her of our unsuccessful attempts to have someone call for pain medication. Patty was as furious as we were. It was not for nothing that we were well-known, not only for our regular visits to take care of Mom, but also for our strong advocacy for her care.

Patty called the nurse on duty and told them that they had one hour to get Mom's pain medication, or she would call 911 to come and take care of Mom. We knew that such action would go on record against the home. Within the hour, Mom had her pain medication. Mary checked on Mom on Sunday, and then headed north to join Patty. I would hold down the fort while they were gone.

When I visited on Monday, Mom was once again in pain, though not as much as Saturday. The directive was only for the weekend, since her doctor had to be contacted once the new week started. Once again she was without relief. "Call her doctor, now!" I demanded. "I am not leaving here until she has the medication she needs." When I was told they couldn't reach the doctor, I said, "I'll stay all night if need be. And I will take further action." I was then told that the doctor on call was making rounds in another part of the building. "Then contact her and tell her to change her route and get down her now! I'll be over helping Mom with lunch when you get the directive."

I consciously shifted my attitude and body language on my way to the table. "Hi, my lovely lady," I said hugging Mom and sitting down next to her. I began cutting up food, feeding her, and helping the other ladies at the table. The lady who always yelled *Help!* and then rattled the table, spilling every-one's beverages to get attention, demanded much of my time this day. I noticed Mom getting irritated at my divided atten-tion, so I would touch her hand or rub her back with one hand while I cut food or rearranged the tray for the other woman.

We were barely done with lunch when the head nurse came over with a slip of paper. "See, we have the order right here. We'll keep it in her file," he said. "I'll get her some pain medication now."

I thanked him, finished helping with lunch, and then visited awhile until Mom got tired.

That incident ran through my mind as I closed the trunk of the car. I thought how fortuitous it was that we had finally gotten the pain medication directive only a couple of weeks before it was imperative that Mom get immediate pain relief. "I'll cancel my trip," I told Patty.

"Don't do that," she said. "They'll be taking X-rays and wheeling her down to physical therapy to see about a reha-bilitation plan." When I hesitated, she added, "I'll call you if there's any change. You're only going to be a couple of hours away."

I decided to go. What I didn't realize was that Patty's plan for rehabilitation was more about her inability to face the fact that Mom was, in all likelihood, not going to recuperate from this fall. I also wanted to believe Patty, that Mom would get better, that we would once again resume our weekly visits. I ignored the nagging voice that whispered *older people die from broken hips*. My traveling companion arrived, parked his car in my garage, and we took off.

We spent a delightful day visiting lifelong friends. We had shared births, deaths, weddings, health, sickness, and more, experiences that bonded us even beyond the separations from moves to distant cities and states, and beyond the busyness of jobs and kids and community events in our own locales.

Now, after over forty years of friendship, we reminisced, shared current events, played cards, ate, and laughed. The next morning we planned to go on a pontoon ride up the Mississippi River, on a warm August day that promised perfect weather, and wildlife sightings. Then I would head home and visit Mom.

The next morning we were just finishing a breakfast of pastries and fruit when Patty called. "You'd better come now. They've never seen anyone fail so fast."

I hung up the phone, apologized unnecessarily, and we took off. The ride home was smooth and quick, even though I rejected the temptation to speed. Less than two hours later, we were pulling into my driveway when Patty called again.

"Don't stop for lunch. She's failing fast."

"I just got home. I'll leave immediately," I told her.

My friend unloaded our luggage from the trunk, said he'd take care of everything and talk to the neighbors who were coming over to greet us. I drove off. As I headed down Highway 169, I decided once again that I would stay focused and drive the speed limit. If I was not meant to see Mom alive again, I had spent many days enjoying her company. I thought of a similar drive when my father had had a stroke and was at North Memorial Hospital. That time I definitely drove over the speed limit crying and yelling at God, "I'm not ready yet! You can't have him!" Dad survived and lived many more years. This time, Mother would not survive. I drove the streets that had become so familiar and parked in my spot right in front of the door. A sign had at one time declared this to be a No Parking Zone. Even though the sign was gone, no one parked there, leaving it open for me. Today, I was grateful for my special spot.

Inside, the hallway looked familiar, yet distant. This would be one of the last times I walked this familiar route. What was once a strange journey into an even stranger ward, what had become a comfortable walk to visit Mom and her new family whom I had come to know and love, was already in the process of becoming memory. Once I walked through the locked doors, I would have to face Mom's death as a concrete reality, not just a phone call. I pushed the red button and walked in.

I stood at the doorway to Mom's room, observing her legacy. Between twenty-five and thirty children, grandchildren and great-grandchildren crowded into her room. Some were silent; others talked in small groups. A hushed background matched Mom's drugged, almost inaudible breathing. Rara and Maia, two of the youngest, sat on either side of their great-grandma on her bed, rubbing lavender lotion into her hands and arms. Patty and Mary stood on either side at the head of her bed.

Patty looked up and saw me. "Barbara's here. Make room so she can get to Mom's bed," she commanded.

Like the parting of the sea, the waves of people moved to either side, making an easy path for me to walk through. I went to the far side of the bed by Patty, who stepped back to let me get closer. I bent down toward Mom, gently brushed her hair back from her temple, and kissed her on her forehead.

"Hello, my lovely lady," I whispered. "I'm sorry you fell. I love you." I kept my hand on her, wanting to do something to comfort her, even though, between her body giving up this life and the deep unconsciousness from the drugs, I couldn't be sure she was aware of anything.

I was talking to my son Louis when Rara looked up at the ceiling and around the room. "What are all of those people doing here with us?" she asked. She looked at her grandmother Patty, who like the rest of us saw nothing. Patty told her that those were angels and friends, waiting to welcome Grandma to the other side. We had often had experiences with our young ones connecting to the other side and had long ago decided to honor their knowing, even when we couldn't experience it.

"And that man there," she continued, pointing to the wedding picture of Dad and Mom we kept on the window ledge, "He's here too, right over there." She pointed to the corner next to my son Louis. Rara, in her youthful innocence, gave me and the others in the room the gift of concretely knowing what many of us felt but still doubted. She also comforted us with a knowing that Mom would not be alone when she made her journey to the other side. Just as we loved her here on earth, others loved and waited for her when she birthed into a new life.

All of a sudden, Mom sat up, a look of terror in her eyes, a half moan, half scream caught in her throat. I rushed to her side while my niece ran to get the nurse. I brushed the side of her hair, caressed her in my arms and shushed her, much like I had done to my children to quiet hurt or fearful tears. "Shh, shh, it will be all right" I whispered. "It will be OK. Shhhh." I thought how much I knew it would not be all right. Yet I kept repeating the same words over and over. If nothing else, their sounds seemed to relax her a bit.

Jesse, the head nurse, rushed in with an eye dropper filled with oxycontin. I stepped back. He gently held her head and put the liquid under her tongue. It seemed to work instantly. I watched him talk to her and assure her the pain would be gone, she would be all right. He rested his hand on her face a moment. Watching him, I could see the love he showed Mom, far beyond simply doing his job. I thought how lucky we were to have Mom spend her last days in this place with so many staff who truly cared for their patients, who truly cared for my mother.

To this day, I often wonder how much of Mom's terror was pain and how much was her deep-seated fear of death. I still picture that panicked, terrified look in her eyes, eyes that still saw none of us, even though they were open. I still remember that helpless feeling, hoping that somehow my shushing made a bit of difference. Perhaps it haunts me because that was the last waking moment I had with my mother. Then, she was gone again, resting in her drug-induced state, physically there, yet farther away than the Alzheimer's had ever before taken her. Even with everyone there, I felt momentarily very alone.

A hospice worker came in with a guitar. We sang old songs and hymns, most of which Mother had enjoyed throughout her life. Music is one of the last parts of the brain to succumb to Alzheimer's. I like to think that Mother somehow heard music that gave her peace in her final moments. I thought of a friend whose mother had been in an Alzheimer's-induced vegetative state for over two years. Still, Mary Jo visited her mother weekly. Shortly before Christmas, on her last visit, she sang Christmas songs that the family had shared around the piano every holiday season. Within a half hour after she had left, her mother died. We talked about what part the music likely had in her passing, what goes on in the many levels of the brain and DNA that we can't begin to comprehend. Like my touches, I hoped that the music would make her passing as gentle and easy as possible.

While we were singing, I looked out at the beautiful August day, the trees swaying in the breeze. Then I saw it. A chrysalis had somehow attached to Mom's window. While we sang, a monarch butterfly emerged and slowly began its first flight.

"Look!" I said, pointing. We all watched the butterfly test its wings before flying away, leaving the empty green chrysalis still hanging from the window. Then we resumed singing. What a beautiful metaphor for the soul leaving the body, I thought. This was by no means a new concept, yet here, watching that butterfly, I understood just how beautiful and free the soul is when it dies to this world and births into the next.

When the hospice worker left, it was close to suppertime, and no one had even had lunch. I emptied my billfold of cash and told Patty to order pizzas and pop for everyone. Others chipped in and we had plenty to go around. Mom's room was at the end of the hall, and the room across the hall was empty. Some of the aides told us to use that as our eating space and brought us paper plates and napkins. The quiet of Mom's room contrasted to the noisy chatter of the kids and adults, who could take a deep breath and resume normal living for a moment. We laughed; we shared remembered stories; we talked about our lives today. We turned a clean nursing home room into a chaos of boxes, plates, napkins, and leftover food. Then, while people went back to Mom to say their final *goodbyes* before leaving, Patty and I shoved everything into huge plastic bags, wiped up spills, and got the room reasonably back to its original state.

We decided that Mary, her daughter Candace, and I would stay and wait for Bob and Sharon to get there. With everyone gone, the quiet of the room caused us to speak in whispers. We drank coffee, occasionally went to talk to Mom, and half rested while we waited.

When Bob and Sharon finally walked in, Mary and I both immediately noticed Sharon's wristband. It read *just when the caterpillar thought all hope was gone, it turned into a beautiful butterfly.* We looked at each other wide-eyed. Then we told Sharon about the butterfly outside Mom's window. It was what we often said was too coincidental to be coincidence. It seemed like we were being given so many gifts while we grieved leaving a mother. It also spoke to our deep connection to each other.

Sharon spent some time with Mom. Then we all said a late-night *goodbye.* I think I might have stayed the night, but Bob and Sharon were going to be staying at my house. We had all had a long, long day. I bent down, kissed Mom, and whispered. "I have to go now. Rest well. There are two angels, one on each side of your bed. They'll watch over you and be with you." I paused, then added, "It's OK if you decide to leave.

We'll all miss you dearly, but we will be OK. If you stay, I will see you in the morning. Otherwise, sweet dreams my lovely lady."

I left my car at Mary's and rode to my house with Bob and Sharon, happy to trade in my hour-long drive for the five-minute one. I'd pick up my car when we came back in the morning.

At 5:30 AM, the phone rang. Even before answering it, I knew what Patty would have to say. "Mom died at 5 o'clock this morning." Bob and Sharon came out of the other bedroom, knowing, yet needing to hear the reality of the words, *she is gone.*

Chapter 20

Funeral Preparations

It was mid-morning, the same day we got Patty's call. We were buying clothes for Mom's funeral. Did I really say we needed to buy her sexy black under pants with white polka dots?

Bob, Sharon, and I stood around the phone in my kitchen in our pajamas in the early dawning morning. I put the phone on speaker so we could all hear the rest of Patty's conversation. "With Labor Day being this weekend, we will have to have the funeral either this Friday or next Tuesday."

I looked at Bob and Sharon and then voiced my vote. "I think we should go for Friday. If we wait till Tuesday, the kids will miss the first day of school and will be too close to the funeral emotionally the rest of the week." Bob and Sharon agreed.

"I agree, too," Patty said. "I'd prefer Friday, but then we'll have to do everything today: the nursing home, the funeral home, the church, flowers, newspaper announcement, all today."

"We can do it. We've done marathons before," I said. We all agreed to go for Friday, settling on a 9:15 AM meeting time at the nursing home. This would be early for Mary, but also doable for her.

Just about everyone I talked to or listened to recommended having funeral arrangements planned in advance. For whatever reason, we hadn't done that. We knew where Mom would be buried, next to Dad in the mausoleum. We had often discussed which church should hold the service, finally agreeing that most, if not all, of those who knew Mom at her original church were no longer alive. Since she had gone to church with Mary most recently, she should be buried at Saint Joseph the Worker. With everything else left to do, we went back to bed for a couple of hours of much-needed rest.

Later, at the nursing home, Bob parked in my usual spot. Once in the ward, our walk to Mom's room was filled with hugs, condolences, assurances of how special Mom was and how much the workers would miss her. I thanked God for leading us to this place and these people, in spite of my former reticence and foot-stomping.

Patty was already in Mom's room, taking down family pictures and mementos to share with other family members. Mary soon joined us. I looked at the pictures on the wall. They had traveled from her home to assisted living, to the nursing home room, ending up here in her Alzheimer's room. Always we hoped to surround her with familiarity and a sense of home, family, and comfort. We looked through her clothes and picked out a mauve pink blouse, a soft, beautiful color on her.

"I refuse to take any of these bras to the funeral home," I said. "I'd be embarrassed to death to have anyone see them." The laundry was hard on all of Mom's clothes, but brutal with her bras. We agreed to get new ones and, while her pants were sort of acceptable, get new pants too. Her blouse was fairly new and would probably look better on her than what we could buy, especially in such a limited amount of time.

A couple of the head nurses came in while we were pondering what to do with Mom's things.

"Can anyone here use Mom's TV or chair, or perhaps her wall hangings and quilts?" I asked them. "Maybe someone could use some of her better clothes?" We all nodded in agreement.

"We could use whatever you want to leave," one of them said. "You'd be surprised how many patients are brought in, left in barren rooms and never visited. We can go through everything, divide it up, and take what we can't use to Goodwill."

We thanked them and left with the few remaining personal possessions Mom had. Our next stop was Catherine's store, where we had bought most of Mom's clothes. We told the clerk what we were looking for and that it was for our mother's funeral.

"I'm so sorry. Honey, you just let me take care of you," the clerk told us. "I've done this many times, even for my mother, and I know what you need." She wrapped her love around us, led us to the bras, and helped us pick out a pair of black pants that set off the mauve color perfectly. We thought we were done, but she added, "They like you to have underpants for the deceased."

I couldn't see why, but I trusted that she knew more than I did. Looking over at a circular table, I spotted a pair of black cotton panties with tiny white dots, kind of like a dotted swiss. "Look at these," I said to everyone. "They are perfect."

My three sisters looked at me like maybe I had snapped from the strain of Mom's death. "She never wore pants like that when she was alive," they all said.

"I bet she wanted to but couldn't let herself," I pleaded. "We can't bury our mother in boring white. I know she'll be looking down and smiling."

Three sisters looked at each other, rolled their eyes in unison, and said, "Whatever. Bring them over and let us pay for everything." Our mom would be special, even in her casket, even if no one but us knew why.

Our next stop was the funeral home. We decided to have visitation before the Mass at the church. We knew the funeral's theme had to have something to do with butterflies and settled on a pamphlet cover with the words, *Just when the caterpillar thought the world was over, it became a butterfly . . .* and on the inside, *A butterfly lit beside us like a sunbeam. And for a brief moment its glory and beauty belonged to our world. Then it flew on again, and though we wish it could have stayed we felt so lucky to have seen it.* We chose a picture of Mom in a hat, remembering earlier days when hats were always worn at church, and because her eyes sparkled and her smile laughed out at us. We added that photo to the left side of the message. Unable to sleep the night before, I had typed the names of all her living and deceased descendants. I had the others double-check it. We then chose a coffin, finalized the details, and were done.

It was lunch time, and we were super hungry. We decided to go to a favorite restaurant of Mom's in Robbinsdale, Nonna Rosa's, which took over when our first favorite restaurant, Thistles, closed. Nonna Rosa's opened in the same location with good Italian food and a less trendy, less pricey menu. It became another favorite. During our meal, we reminisced, told family tales, told Mom tales, laughed, got teary eyed, and occasionally got quiet, each in our own thoughts. It was a time to grieve, a time to celebrate Mom's life, a time to comfort one another.

Our next stop was the church office. We began by telling the woman our butterfly story and proceeded to the more complex task of planning the ceremony. Our usual animated discussions and the give-and-take we'd mastered throughout Mom's illness were in evidence here.

"I think we should start out with *On Eagle's Wings*," suggested Sharon.

"Don't you think that *Lord of the Dance* would be a better processional song, sort of like God inviting Mom and us to dance with Him?" I countered.

Knowing my love of dance, Sharon acquiesced. "OK, but then we have *On Eagle's Wings* as the Communion song." Deal.

And so it went with all of us feeling free to ask for what was important to us and willing to let go of what mattered less. By the time we had finished, it was late afternoon. We had one more stop, my niece's flower shop, Addie Lane, in Blaine.

"I'm so tired, I really don't want to drive that far," yawned Mary.

"Me, either," said Patty.

"Would you trust Sharon and me to pick out the flowers?" I asked.

They were more than ready to call it a day and gave us the go ahead to pick out what we thought would look nice. Bob, Sharon and I headed for the flower shop, which was on our way home, after goodbyes and arrangements to check in with each other the next day.

Miki greeted us with her usual animation, gave a few suggestions, and then left us to look around the shop for ideas. We first looked at potted plants and toyed with the idea of combining them with cut flowers for one arrangement. Then we went into the cooler to see what appealed to us. We both loved the pinks and lavenders, with some yellow for bright color. Mom's favorite flower was pink roses so we knew those were a must; I loved the soft orchid look of Alstroemeria. With vague ideas in mind, we settled onto the couch in the corner of the shop and began to look at books of arrangements for the casket. Sharon would *kind of like* one, and I would *kind of like* another, but never the same one. Our tastes were direct opposites. Once, we had made a healing blanket for Patty when she was really sick. We considered it a miracle when we finally, after more than an hour, had settled on a material that we both liked. Making the blanket was nothing compared to shopping for the materials. Here we were again.

I turned a page and we both said, "This is it." The arrangement looked like a summer garden with flowers of all colors. It was lush and beautiful. Perhaps our taste wasn't so opposite after all. We called Miki over, showed her the picture, told her we wanted the top cut back because of the open casket, and proceeded to look for the flowers from the grandchildren. I also wanted a bouquet from her brother, who was in Florida and unable to come to the funeral. I hadn't had a chance to talk to him, but I was ready to pay for the flowers myself so he could in some way be part of the services. We decided on a huge basket combining plants and flowers from the grand-children, and a huge vase with coordinating flowers from her brother. We picked out a heart of fourteen pink roses, each rose representing a great or great-great grandchild, to be placed inside the casket by her. Knowing our butterfly story, Miki showed us some silk butterflies to add to the arrange-ments. We left the final details up to her and headed home, exhausted but self-satisfied after finishing our marathon. Bob had stayed in the background to once again watch the Lefaive girls somehow weave their differences into a masterpiece!

Chapter 21

Mom's Funeral

It was a juxtaposition of grieving a loss and celebrating a life. Butterflies and dance wove through the ceremony reminding me of the best times Mom and I had together. In The Voice of the Master, Kahlil Gibran says that tears and laughter come and go throughout our lives. Today we had both.

When I walked toward Mom's casket, the first thing I noticed was a myriad of flowers, like a meadow of colorful summer blossoms with butterflies flitting about. Several of my groups of friends, my bridge group, my river ladies, my townhomes association, and others had ordered their flowers from Addie Lane. Butterflies rested in all of those arrangements. The spray of flowers on the coffin was more beautiful than the picture we had chosen, pink roses peeking out from every flower of every color that was in season. The heart of thirteen pink roses rested in the coffin by her head. So much beauty and life, such a contrast to the death we were experiencing, and yet such a celebration of Mom's life and her birthing into a new life.

I thought of a dream I'd had several years earlier. In it I sat on a hill covered with wildflowers, holding an old woman. She had asked me to bring her to this place to die. She lay in my arms while we watched the afternoon sun become sunset. *Bury me in this beautiful place*, she whispered. At the end of the dream, I was visiting her grave on the same hill. The church narthex was no hill, but Mom was certainly being buried amongst the beauty of flowers.

I stood looking at Mom. The peaceful expression on her face showed no sign of the difficult life she had lived. I had prayed that Alzheimer's would not lock her into horrific memories of her past. If any of those memories did come, they were fleeting, leaving her to experience joy and love for and from all around her. Someone had painted her nails a soft pink. So many times I had painted those nails, a pampering she enjoyed throughout her life. The pearls I had brought to the funeral home on Thursday were a testament to the jewelry she wore and loved to the end.

I thought of the complex relationship we'd had throughout our lives. I'd had to let go of Mom first through therapy to be able to accept her in whatever way she could interact. How strange that my abuse growing up gave me a compassion for others that allowed me not only to see their difficulties and help them, but also to see their strength in the methods they devised to survive. I eventually turned that compassion toward Mom, honoring her struggles in her life and honoring the talents she used to express her love and strength. However, it was the Alzheimer's, that horrendous, devastating disease, that gave us more moments of joy and love than in Mom's cognizant life. While the disease ravaged her brain, it also destroyed most of the depression and mental illness that had plagued her. It took away her expectations for me that I could never fulfill. Wisdom, I had read, was the ability to hold opposites in your brain and still maintain your sanity. Perhaps I could one day share the bits of wisdom that I had garnered from this journey to help others on their own difficult paths. But that was for another day. For now, I was content and at peace with the life Mom and I had shared, and I was feeling quite sane.

Patty came up to stand next to me. "She actually looks happy," she said.

"It's the black panties," I answered. "She's giggling about them."

We both chuckled and moved on. The usual hugs and condolences filled the time before the Mass. I was not one to cry
and emote in public, becoming calm and almost stoic in the
face of trauma. I had handled my kids' trips to the emergency
room for stitches with such apparent ease, that my friends marveled at me. They didn't see the alone tears and shaking that
came later. Good or bad, that was me; I would be quite calm
now, almost like a hostess. While there would be quiet tears,
most of my grieving would come privately, later. In the midst
of all the interactions, my grandson-in-law came up to me and
held me, not a hug, but wrapping his arms around me. For a
few minutes, it felt so good to relax into his love and caring. I
rested my head on his shoulder and quietly thanked him.

I noticed Patti in the crowd, a woman who had worked at
Mom's assisted living residence. She had built a special relationship with Mom, who came to visit her daily at her desk.
Patti visited Mom regularly in the nursing home, far beyond
what a caregiver would normally do. I walked over to her and
thanked her for coming. "I was so afraid I would miss her
funeral," she said. "I am glad I saw her obituary in the paper. I
can't stay for the Mass. We're going out of town. I just needed
to say a final goodbye."

She told me about her own mother's recent death and
started to cry. I was well aware of how a funeral can tie into
many previous ones. I held her and told her how sorry I was
for her loss. Here we were, two women who really didn't know
each other, brought momentarily closer by a similar loss. Then
she walked out the door, and I knew I would probably never
see her again. Still, she had played such a vital role in Mom's
life while she slipped ever deeper into her private world of
Alzheimer's.

I turned to see the priest walking towards me. Only the
greatest sense of propriety kept my mouth from hanging open.
A three-foot orange monarch butterfly adorned the front of

his cream-colored vestment. "I bought this for special occasions," he said, after initial handshakes. "I think this is just the perfect one."

I agreed, adding how beautiful it was, and how majestic to have just a single, large butterfly.

"I think we will move the funeral to the side chapel. It's smaller and more intimate. Is that all right with you?"

"I think it's a good idea," I concurred. Then he moved on to make final preparations for the Mass.

I don't know whether I was lost in reverie, simply looking in another direction, or as I often do, tuning out what was going on around me, aware of its happening, but not being directly connected. "Barbara," Sharon said. "It's time. We're going in."

I found myself being escorted to the front of the processional line, directly behind the coffin. My preference would have been to be at the back of the line, to become one with the crowd, not the center of attention. However, our family had its protocols. "You are the matron of the family now," my niece had said when we were talking. As the oldest, I was to be first, with my daughter Christine and son Louis on either side of me, the rest of my family directly behind us. The other families lined up by age. This all took but moments before the ushers began slowly moving the casket forward. The music began, the song "Lord of the Dance". *Dance, dance, wherever you may be, I am the Lord of the dance, said He . . . won't you come and dance with me?* I pictured Mom, dancing in heaven. I was torn between the solemnity of the procession and wanting to dance my way into the church, dancing, if you will, once again, with Mom.

"I want this song at my funeral," I whispered to Christine.

The side chapel was a perfect size for us. We formed a *U* shape around the casket, the people in the front row almost close enough to touch the coffin if they stretched out their hands. I was in a seat at the end of one of the side rows, holding my great-granddaughter, Calli, who was crying. She had seen me teary-eyed which in turn, had started her tears. The rituals of the Mass were comforting, allowing me to participate or drift off at times. Then came the homily.

Father talked about being in a butterfly tent at the State Fair, butterflies on and everywhere around him. He told how the caterpillar winds the chrysalis and then dissolves into a green liquid. When the butterfly emerges, its DNA is different from the caterpillar, a miraculous, inexplicable scientific miracle! He compared that to our own death and resurrection into a new, more beautiful life. How perfect, I thought. We are not at all what we were here on earth, yet we take with us what we experienced on our earth journey. He talked about how, in an experiment, caterpillars were shocked every time they were introduced to a certain smell. They were soon repelled by that smell, even without the shock. When the butterfly emerged from its chrysalis, it, too, was repelled by that smell. I felt like I really understood the transition into another life, whether it is called *heaven* or any of the other names different religions give such passing. I can't say I understood it mentally, but rather that I had a knowing that accepted the unexplainable complexities of this mystery.

After Mass, we had a meal prepared by the ladies of the church.

"Did you order these flowers?" my good friend Kitty asked. On each table was a sprig of Alstroemeria, my favorite flower.

"No," I answered. "We had nothing to do with the meal planning." Serendipity struck again!"

After socializing and saying *goodbye* to everyone, our family went to the cemetery to bury Mom next to Dad. Their crypt was at the top of the mausoleum. I remember when Dad was lifted into it, I had said we should all sing *Nearer My*

God to Thee, my weird sense of humor showing up. It seemed appropriate now too. A hoist raised the casket with a man on either side. As they tried to slip the casket in, it caught. I had visions of it toppling down, Mom rolling out of it. Finally, they worked out the kinks and slid the casket smoothly into place next to Dad's. It was all over. We stood around talking or wandered the grounds, admiring the lush gardens that were still in bloom. All of the intensity and rushing of the last few days were over. The funeral had been what we had hoped for. "It was more like a celebration than a funeral," a friend had told me. Indeed, we had chosen to honor Mom's life, not her long progression toward death, with the songs we chose, the butterfly theme, and the brightly colored flowers. And, we felt, we had succeeded.

We agreed to meet at Mary's the next day for a barbecue. We all felt the need to do something casual, something we had done countless times before. Still, I knew that in the midst of the normalcy was the reality that both of our parents were gone. The words *you are now the matriarch* were a testimony to that reality. My life, my role in the family, had changed as had that of every one of us.

"I miss you already, Mom," I whispered as I walked to my car and got in. "Goodbye, my lovely lady."

Afterword

When Mom died in late August of 2013, we sisters could never have imagined that six and a half years later we would be hearing words like *pandemic, shelter in place, COVID-19.* Likewise, we had no inkling of how those words would affect us, and how they would cause us to revisit Mom's Alzheimer's.

I woke up the morning of March 13, 2020 an active, vital 78-year-old woman. I got up early three mornings a week for a high intensity water aerobics class; on Monday afternoons, I did a Pilates Reformer workout for core strength; I worked several nights a week at a dance studio, ending Tuesdays with an adult clogging class. I socialized with friends over lunch and cards, belonged to a book club, and had finished writing my first book. Patty, Mary, and I met two or more times a month to assure that Mother's death would not be the end of our closeness. Together we visited Sharon and Bob several times a year. COVID-19 was news, but in distant places like China and Italy. Even New York seemed distant. Rumors of it coming to Minnesota were whispered, but we couldn't believe it could reach the pandemic stage in our Upper Midwest state.

Then the 5 o'clock news shattered any illusions of safety. For the first time I heard the words *shelter in place.* "We must protect those around us who are vulnerable, especially the elderly."

"Yes," I agreed, thinking about my friends in senior and assisted living apartments.

Governor Tim Walz continued, "We must protect those over sixty and, more importantly, the elderly over seventy."

I again agreed. "Yes . . . oh shit! That's me!" That is when it hit me that I was considered vulnerable because of my age; all of my efforts to stay healthy countered by that one number, *78.*

While the pandemic didn't affect me in terms of contracting a virus, it did leave an indelible mark on my life. A shadow had been forming on my left eye. My plan to see my eye doctor on Monday, March 16, ended when all businesses were closed, including eye clinics. At first I tried to be optimistic. I could wait for two weeks. Then when two weeks were added to the shutdown, I braced myself for yet another delay. My eyesight kept getting worse. Sometimes I saw double; sometimes straight lines became distorted; always there was that shadow.

With talk of yet another extension of the shutdown, I called the clinic's emergency number. The nurse told me to try home remedies for a week, consisting mainly of hot packs and eye drops, both of which I had regularly used when my eyes were dry or tired. Still, I complied. During the next week and a half my vision kept deteriorating. I called again and finally got an appointment with a doctor on April 27, six weeks after my planned examination.

Sitting in the room with the nurse, I began my usual appointment with the eye chart assessment. Looking at the chart through my left eye, the reality of how bad it really was took my breath away, literally. My right eye had done its usual grand job reading the bottom line of letters. Perfect vision, excellent physical condition. My left eye also showed equally well in the physical tests. However, the bottom two thirds of the chart were completely black; the huge top line so distorted I had to concentrate to even attempt a single letter.

I sat waiting for the doctor, hoping for the best, fearing the worst. I had reason to dread the possibility of it being my macula. I had watched my father go blind from macular degeneration, week by week, year by year. In my last memory, a few weeks before he died, we sat in the annex of a church where my grandson, his great-grandson was being baptized. I described everything that was happening in detail so he could envision the ceremony in his mind's eye. *Will you introduce me to everyone when we talk?* he whispered. *I can't see who they are, only shadows.* It is one thing to make life as normal and manageable as possible for someone you love. It is a totally different reality to imagine that future for yourself.

I couldn't sit still anymore, imagining the worst, fighting back tears. I got up and started to do my leg stretches that I always did before and after my dance classes. I took my sandals off and with my right heel out in front of me, stretched my calf muscles, always tight from years of clogging. Then I stretched my leg back, feeling my thigh muscles complain a bit, then relax. My left leg was next. I sat back down and leaned forward, one ankle on top of the opposite knee, stretching out each glute, the big butt muscle that got ever bigger as I aged. Physical concentration worked; I relaxed a bit. No more tears. We would do what we could to fix whatever we could.

I quickly put my sandals back on when I heard the door open. I had had Dr. Eggeman before. He was pleasant, reassuring. Still, he could not promise my sight would return to normal. *We can improve your eyesight. However, it will not be as good as it previously was.* He explained that blood was pooling on the macula. When he further explained that it was *druzied*, I almost had to laugh. My daughter had given me a beautiful necklace the year before. One stone was druzied black quartz. I had no idea what that meant, so I looked it up. *The rough surface of the stone was created over thousands of years by moisture dripping on the rock, creating a pocked surface.* I had a perfect vision of what my macula must look like, thinking *It is much prettier on a stone.* He made an appointment with a specialist. The soonest I could get in was a week later.

All I could think of that night was how much damage had been done while I *sheltered in place*; how much better my sight could have been if six weeks of progression had been only days. I was angry at myself for not noticing what I now knew were early signs. I was angry at having to do a home trial because of the pandemic. Mostly I was angry at the pandemic, that elusive monster that changed my life overnight, more than ever with my damaged left eye. *That gd mf pandemic!* I railed while talking to my daughter, using language that seldom came out of my mouth, language that my grandmother would have said *would make a sailor blush*. I cried, a lot, thinking, *If I could cry into a hole in my backyard, I could live on ocean-front property*. Finally, I calmed down and prepared to face the next week like I had faced the pandemic: get up, do morning yoga, plan a project for the day, and go for walks. The dark cloud of losing my eyesight hung over me like the dark cloud of the coronavirus hung over our state, country, and world.

Another haunting thought slipped in. If I had signs of my father's macular degeneration, what about my mother's Alzheimer's? What would the effect of isolation, walks instead of workouts, the stress of a drastic change in my life be on my brain, not just my mental state? I shook off both thoughts. I would continue to walk, I would enjoy my dance class on zoom, and I would do yoga. And I would wait for my next appointment, hoping that a specialist could undo some of the damage to my eye.

While I waited, Mary called me one night. "Please pray for Sue's mother. She is isolated in an Alzheimer's ward and so confused about why no one comes to see her or touch her." Sue was a lifelong friend who was like another sister to Mary. Sue's frequent visits, like ours had, included treats and touching. She now could talk through the first floor window, but that outside world was way too distant a reality. I thought of the woman in Mom's ward who would stand in front of a window as if it were a wall, interacting with some past memory, oblivious to the outside world of trees and flowers. I thought of how I would disappear from Mom's reality if I even sat too far away.

"Sue feels so guilty for not bringing her home, but she has to work. She can't afford daycare. You'd better pray for Sue too. Can you imagine what it would be like if we couldn't have visited Mom? I don't know what I would have done."

I promised Mary I would pray for Sue and her mom, and we reminisced about fun times with our mom. After this, I decided to focus on those with problems much worse than mine. I knew that whatever happened, I would be OK. I was good at adapting.

After a repeat of the eye tests and X-rays, I met Dr. Peterson. He proved to be an amazing doctor. He explained what was happening in my left eye, showing me the X-rays of first my right eye with its normal curves and veins. My left eye, in contrast, showed a mountainous blob to the left surrounded by a tangle of veins. In the middle of the macula was a huge red blob of blood from the leaking veins.

I was devastated.."How fast will this progress?" I asked, trying to keep my voice steady. "Will it affect my driving?" I thought of my less-than-a-year-old fun Rav 4. "If I need to move to an apartment, I want to be proactive. I don't want my children having to make tough decisions because I refused to make them."

"You have many years of driving ahead of you," he reassured me. "Your right eye is in excellent condition and will help you see well." That was Dr. Peterson's style, thorough, professional, yet relaxed and comforting. I felt confident in his care.

Dr. Peterson explained that our first job was to reduce the inflammation. He would conduct a series of four monthly shots, starting that day, in my left eye, which would stop the progression and hopefully restore some of my sight. I pictured a long huge needle coming toward my eye and me either passing out or throwing up. Then he went step-by-step, explaining what would happen, first assuring me that I wouldn't even see the needle because it went into the outside corner of my eye.

"First I will put a numbing gel on your eye three times with a few minutes in between. I will insert a spring between your eyelids so you don't have to worry about blinking. You will feel a slight pressure while I measure your eye and then a twinge with the shot."

I leaned back in the chair, ready to do whatever it took to maintain my precious eyesight. I did my deep breathing, the kind I do when meditating or during yoga, and sent healing energy to my left eye. The gel, the spring, then, *now you will feel a slight pressure.* The pressure proved to be a sharp pain, lasting about two seconds.

"We're done," Dr. Peterson said. The shot was much easier and quicker than I could have imagined, the brief pain less than if I had stubbed my toe. He then told me that for a few days I would see black dots toward the bottom of my vision. "That is the medicine. It will absorb in two or three days."

The dots were fluid like, about the size of a dime or nickel. What was most fun was that they looked like they were outside my eye. I would lift my food to my mouth, the dots would appear, and I would quickly shift my hand to the right and put the food in sideways on the right side. Anyone watching would deem me stranger than usual because there really was nothing in front of me. I simply laughed, corrected my trajectory for that time, and then instinctively did the same thing again at my next meal.

Mary called again that week. "You won't believe what the nursing home did now," she ranted. "Someone got the virus, so they took everything out of every room, including chairs and televisions. They told Sue it could be a couple of weeks before her mom gets anything back . . . She can't leave her room; she is in solitary confinement without even TV to distract her."

"What!?" I said. "They can disinfect the chair and TV in her room. It would take a lot less time than moving everything. It sounds totally inhumane to me."

"They took her doll too. You remember Mom. Those dolls are their babies."

"Remember when there was a flu going through Mom's ward?" I said. "They disinfected everything. Her rubber ball turned into this hard mass. It took forever to find another one, but they got her doll back to her the next day. They were so caring toward Mom." I promised to continue to pray for both Sue and her mother.

The next night, Mary gave me an update. "Sue put up such a fuss, they brought her mom's TV and chair back to her room. They promised to get the doll back within a day or two."

"That's great," I said, "but it shouldn't take a complaint to think about the human needs of their residents." I thought of another friend whose mother was rapidly regressing mentally and physically in her nursing home confinement. In spite of good care, the lack of weekly visits was taking a toll. I thought of a friend who had barely been out of her apartment for almost three months, even having her meals delivered to her. I thought of how my own mental sharpness seemed to be fuzzier lately, one day blending into the previous and the next.

Many psychologists who have been interviewed on news programs have speculated about a spike in mental illness, most likely PTSD (post traumatic stress disorder), when the distancing and isolation ends. I have often wondered if there would be a similar spike in dementia cases. When Mary visited a ninety-year-old neighbor through her screen door, the woman said, "You will have to excuse me; my words come a bit slow. I haven't talked to anyone for so long, I can't always remember the words right away." Then, when Mary told her she had brought Barb's mint brownies, the woman's tears changed to a big smile. "She had a sparkle in her eyes," Mary told me. How little it takes to brighten a dull day, or month, or many months. How important to remember how something that seems so little to us can mean so much to someone else. I'd like to think that it might even help ward off dementia. At the very least, it can make one part of one day special.

When I went in for my second shot, I knew what to expect and was much more relaxed. The pictures of my left eye were much improved. The swelling had diminished and a small light-pink area showed where the large, dark-red one had been. I still often saw double or distorted images, but we had several shots to go. Perhaps I was a bit too relaxed. My weird sense of humor kicked in. "Before I forget, I would like you to write me a prescription for a pedicure."

Dr. Peterson looked at my toes, looked up at me and said, "What?!"

I explained that when I had tried to do my own pedicure that week, I often missed my toenails and painted my toes or the surrounding area and had to really concentrate. I would often miss the jar on my first attempt to put the brush back in for more polish. I later had to let a couple of showers wash the excess polish off my toes. "I consider that a medical emergency," I told him.

"Where do you want it?" he quipped.

It was my turn to say, "What?"

"Barbados or the Bahamas. Which one would you like for your pedicure?"

"I like the way you think," I laughed.

Dr. Peterson was serious and professional with explanations or during a procedure. He also knew the value of light hearted human interaction to make that procedure less stressful. Or . . . perhaps his sense of humor was a wee bit like mine!

The pandemic has taught each one of us how life can suddenly change. It has also given us a lot of time to think, sometimes more than I would like. "As each of us sisters ages," Patty told me the other day, "we worry more that Mom's Alzheimer's might be hereditary. We worry that senior moments might be the start of something much more serious." We agreed that while it is often in the back of our minds, worrying won't help anything. Then, as we did so often, we reminisced about Mom: about her wild storytelling, about her singing *You Are My Sunshine* with us, about her many sewn creations which are now momentos for us.

We sisters have taken so many trips down memory lane, both painful and happy. It has been a wondrous journey for all of us. As I now start my next journey with macular degeneration, a word that still feels strange in my mouth, I wake each morning with a prayer of gratitude for the beauty of a new day and end with a prayer of thanks for that day. And . . . I still keep dancing!

My most recent performance was on a platform on the north parking lot of the dance studio with a seascape backdrop covering the entire wall. Each class came at a separate time to keep the numbers within the pandemic guidelines. When our turn came, I was so excited to see everyone, I almost forgot about social distancing. Then I restrained myself. Each of us women walked out to our taped out space. We smiled at each other, the music started, and then we danced. A few parents from the previous class stayed to watch, sitting in chairs on the lawn. The sun shone down on us. The breeze cooled us. Nothing, not the shadow of Alzheimer's, not the shadow of macular degeneration, not even the shadow of a pandemic could dull the joy I felt dancing surrounded by friends! That feeling of joy is what motivates me to keep dancing through the storms in my life. Then, when I wake up each morning, I can breathe in the fresh air and say, "Life is good."

Time Line of Mom's Alzheimer's

May 25, 2004   Mom moves to Waterford.

June 9, 2004   I retire to give me more time with Mom.

April, 2007   We rent a hall for Mom's 85th birthday; people from 1940s to present come to celebrate.

Sept, 2007   Mom's dementia worsens; the doctor from hell prescribes a black flagged drug.

Dec, 2007   Mom spends her last Christmas at Waterford.

Jan 1, 2008   Mom is taken to North Memorial Hospital while I am at Sharon's in Illinois.

Jan 2, 2008   Mom is moved to Northridge; the doctors won't let her go back to her apartment.

Aug, 2008   Mom asks Mary if Dad has died.

Jan 1, 2010   Mom speaks poetic verse in a trance.

March 12, 2010   Mom is moved to Alzheimer's unit.

April, 2011   Mom's 89th birthday is held in the Alzheimer's party room.

2011/12   We sisters attend care meetings about Mom's regression; Mom rages at Mary.

2012   On Memorial Day we sisters lunch with Mom.

Feb, 21012   Mom and I dance.

April 2012   Mom celebrates her 90th birthday in the Alzheimer's ward party room.

Nov. 2012	We sisters continue to meet with Dr. Faber.
April 2013	Mom's 91st birthday is held in the Alzheimer's party room.
August 2013	Mom falls, and breaks her hip; the family gathers.Mom dies at age 91. We sisters plan Mom's funeral to celebrate her life.

Made in the USA
Las Vegas, NV
14 February 2021

17872864R00118